THE WOMEN WHO BUILT HOLLYWOOD

12 TRAILBLAZERS IN FRONT OF AND BEHIND THE CAMERA

SUSAN GOLDMAN RUBIN

CALKINS CREEK

AN IMPRINT OF ASTRA BOOKS FOR YOUNG READERS

New York

For information about permission to reproduce selections from this book, please contact
permissions@astrapublishinghouse.com.

Calkins Creek
An imprint of Astra Books for Young Readers,
a division of Astra Publishing House
astrapublishinghouse.com
Printed in China

ISBN: 978-1-6626-8010-6 (hc)
ISBN: 978-1-6626-8011-3 (eBook)
Publisher's Cataloging-in-Publication data
Names: Rubin, Susan Goldman, author. | Carter, Ruth E., foreword author.
Title: The women who built Hollywood : 12 trailblazers in front of and the behind the
camera / by Susan Goldman Rubin; foreword by Ruth E. Carter.
Description: Includes bibliographical references and index. | New York, NY: Calkins
Creek, an imprint of Astra Books for Young Readers, 2023.
Identifiers: LCCN: 2021925701 | ISBN: 9781662680106 (hardcover) | 9781662680113
(ebook)
Subjects: LCSH Women in motion pictures. | Motion picture actors and actresses—
United States—Biography. | Women in the motion picture industry—United States—
History. | Motion pictures—United States—History. | BISAC YOUNG ADULT
NONFICTION / Biography & Autobiography / Women | YOUNG ADULT NONFICTION /
Biography & Autobiography / Performing Arts | YOUNG ADULT NONFICTION /
Performing Arts / Film Classification: LCC PN1995.9.W6 .R83 2023 | DDC
791.43/6522/092—dc23

First edition
10 9 8 7 6 5 4 3 2 1

Designed by Barbara Grzeslo
The text is set in Avenire LT Std.
The titles are set in Anna ITC Std.

Title page: A premiere of *All This, and Heaven Too* at the Fox Carthay Circle Theatre,
Hollywood, California, 1940

To Peter Goldman and Paul Camp,
and in memory of Stephen B. Moldof (1946–2020)
—*SGR*

CONTENTS

A NOTE ON TERMS AND SUBJECTS USED IN THIS BOOK

This anthology reflects the period of history in which the featured filmmakers lived. I used the words "Negro" and "colored" because those are the words Black actresses chose for themselves at the time. With great respect I have quoted their words and those of their colleagues.

The early period of moviemaking reflected discrimination in all levels of American society. Talented Black filmmakers—struggling against racial stereotypes—mainly worked outside of the growing field. Chinese Americans tried to make themselves visible as real people rather than as caricatures.

I have chosen twelve capable, hardworking women from different backgrounds and interests to tell the story of pioneering females in film.

FOREWORD

In 2019, I was honored to become the first African American to win the Academy Award for Costume Design for my work in Marvel Studios' *Black Panther*. The map to becoming the "first," or for anyone desiring an impactful career in any category of filmmaking, was charted by some of the significant contributions made by the diverse group of *The Women Who Built Hollywood*.

During both World War I (1914–1918) and World War II (1939–1945), while men were away fighting in service of their country, women contributed by working in support of the war effort. Women were charged with maintaining life at home and in doing so built much of America across many industries. Part of that work was in the entertainment field. While film was in its infancy and women filmmakers were too, they still boldly took the reins, developing stories that were by and about women. With the craft of filmmaking being so new, women in Hollywood showed, whether it be acting, directing, screenwriting, editing, or costume design, that their point of view was included and this industry was not just for men. Women were creators of story and entertainment. Over time, as men came back from the wars, society relegated a woman's role to being that of a housewife. Women filmmakers had their contributions toward building Hollywood underestimated and overlooked. Yet, they continued to dream bigger than the limitations placed on them.

I can only imagine the strength of character of each woman described in this book and the fortitude it took to dodge insults and endure criticism while confronting gender and racial bias. These women had strong senses of themselves and that confidence

7

guided them in finding a place in this new world that rejected their independence. There was insurmountable bravery on display in what they achieved by being who they were and who they became during their time in building and growing Hollywood. As they succeeded they were able to invite other women into the fold and expand opportunity that once was not there for many of them.

What connects me to these women beyond being a filmmaker is that they were activists. The act of being and expressing themselves was a protest as well as their efforts to rid this country of the foulness of segregation. These women did not just build Hollywood, they contributed to its longevity. They were breaking ground and breaking stereotypes. They were role models. They were a founding generation of women in Hollywood who helped future generations not only exist but have the powerful and diverse voices that they have now. Without Hattie McDaniel, there wouldn't be a Whoopi Goldberg. Without Fredi Washington, there wouldn't be an Angela Bassett or Halle Berry. Without Louise Beavers, there wouldn't be a Viola Davis or an Octavia Spencer. Without Anna May Wong, there wouldn't be a Michelle Yeoh. Without Clare West, there wouldn't have been an Edith Head. And, without Dorothy Arzner, there wouldn't be an Ava DuVernay.

The contributions of the women, as described in this book, built Hollywood and created its legacy. Because they dared to dream, I was able to dream.

Ruth E. Carter
Academy Award-Winning Costume Designer
Marvel Studios' *Black Panther*

INTRODUCTION

In the early days of Hollywood, an amazingly large number of female filmmakers existed. "The doors were wide open to women," wrote a film historian. From 1900 till the 1920s, women not only acted in movies, but they also directed, produced, edited, wrote screenplays, designed costumes, performed stunts, and ran their own companies.

At that time, moviemaking wasn't taken seriously as a business that would make money, so women grabbed opportunities to work in this new industry. They helped one another and kept the movie business thriving as films evolved from silents to talkies. Pioneering filmmakers experimented with modern equipment as they created entertainment for eager audiences.

Reportedly, the first motion picture camera had been invented by Thomas Edison in 1890, and people viewed his images through a peephole. Just a few years later, he promoted the Vitascope to project images on a screen, and audiences panicked as *Sea Waves* rushed toward them. In France, the Lumière brothers created the Cinématographe, and their film of a train hurtling out of the screen scared audiences who ducked and screamed. Filmmakers took to the idea of moving pictures and started telling stories.

The early silent movies called "flickers" were short one- and two-reelers. A single reel of film ran through a projector for eleven minutes and was displayed on a large screen. In America, the moving images appealed to millions of immigrants who couldn't read or understand English. Connecting the written title cards with the movements of the actors helped them learn the language.

They enjoyed the stories of familiar neighborhood types—policemen, gangsters, and laundrywomen. Many more refined people detested the flickers because they considered the content crude. Stage actors looked down on moviemaking as "a complete disgrace," a sure sign of failure for out-of-work performers who needed to earn some money. Compared to the theater, flickers seemed like a cheap form of entertainment. And it was. Nickelodeons were set up in empty storefronts filled with chairs. The name came from the price of admission, a nickel.

However, as short one- and two-reel films became longer features, screenings were moved from noisy nickelodeons to movie palaces. These luxurious "temples of the silent drama" were furnished with rugs, chandeliers, statues, and mirrors to attract middle-class white women who might bring their husbands to the movies for a nice night out worth the price of an expensive ticket. Ladies sipped tea in the women's lounge. Uniformed ushers showed viewers to their plush seats. Female writers and directors created appealing stories.

With the invention of machinery that could record sound, a different style of movie appeared on the screen. Talkies began to replace silents in the late 1920s. The addition of sound transformed the look of movies. The art of the silent film was over. Companies grew larger and more competitive. The movie industry became big business headed by male executives and the studio system began. The "Big Five" studios—MGM, Paramount, Warner Brothers, Fox, and RKO—controlled every aspect of production in the 1930s and 1940s.

Yet ambitious women filmmakers pursued their careers during these changes as well as the epic events of the time: the women's suffrage movement (1848–1920), the Chinese Exclusion Act (1882–1943), the Jim Crow era (1890s–1964), World War I (1914–1918), the Spanish flu pandemic (1918–1920), and the Great Depression (1929–1933). Women carried on to make Hollywood known throughout the world. Who were these remarkable women who loved making movies and built Hollywood?

Mary Pickford, the adorable heroine of *The Poor Little Rich Girl*, 1917

CHAPTER 1 MARY PICKFORD

"DURING A PICTURE, I DIDN'T LEAVE THE CHARACTER AT THE STUDIO; I TOOK IT HOME WITH ME. I LIVED MY PARTS."

—Mary Pickford

The silent movie *The Poor Little Rich Girl* opens with actress Mary Pickford in the title role scampering down the staircase of a mansion. Hoping for a smile, she skips along the hallway to the butlers who tower over her. But they stand stiffly and ignore her.

In this 1917 movie, Mary convincingly played an eleven-year-old, the first of many child roles that made her famous. At the time of filming she was actually twenty-five and earning a million dollars for a movie produced by her own company. Known as "the girl with curls," and "America's Sweetheart," Mary was brilliant in business affairs and became the most powerful and influential woman who ever worked in Hollywood.

Mary Pickford was born in Toronto, Canada, on April 8, 1892. Her given name was Gladys Louise Smith. She was just five when her father died, leaving the family penniless. Her mother Charlotte felt helpless, but Mary was determined to take her father's place and protect her family. Charlotte rented rooms to boarders and one of them, a stage manager, offered to cast Mary and her younger sister Lottie in a play. Like most people, Charlotte regarded theater folk as lowlifes. Yet she desperately needed money and agreed to let her "innocent babies" perform. Mary later claimed that she made her stage debut at age five, but according to biographers she was seven.

At age nine, Mary received an offer to go on tour acting in a play. Charlotte insisted that she, Lottie, and little brother, Jack, be given jobs and go with her. During the next five years, the family traveled from city to city, sitting up all night on trains. With little schooling, Mary said she learned to read from billboards.

As Mary toured, she envied girls in the audience who had fancy clothes and jewelry. "When I saw things that other girls had," she said, "I determined to have them. I'd work for them."

Between engagements, the Smiths stopped in New York and once shared an apartment with the Gish family, which was also fatherless. Mary Gish's daughters Lillian and Dorothy were child actors, too. Lillian and Mary became close friends, but because Mary was a year older than Lillian, she became the leader of the group. "There was never any question when she told us to do something," remembered Lillian, "we did it."

In New York, Mary wangled a meeting with famed theatrical producer and director David Belasco. Upon learning her name, he said, "We'll have to find another." She suggested some family names—Key, Kirby, Pickford. . . . And he said, "Well, my little friend, from now on your name will be Mary Pickford." Her whole family adopted the new last name. Backstage, Belasco introduced her to the leading lady of his play. Mary swooned over the gorgeous dressing room with a star nailed to the door. Someday, she vowed, she would have that dressing room.

Belasco hired her, and on December 3, 1907, at age fifteen, she premiered on Broadway in the play *The Warrens of Virginia*. After the show closed, Belasco had no parts for her although he believed she had "a promising future."

Mary needed to make money. Her mother gingerly suggested that she apply for work at the Biograph Studios, a major movie company. The movie business had started on the East Coast with Biograph located in Manhattan.

"Oh, no, not that, Mama!" cried Mary. Movies were beneath her.

"Only to tide us over," persuaded her mother, "to keep . . . the family together."

Mary, decked out in high heels, her best blue suit, and a new straw hat, resentfully went to the Biograph building. As she climbed the stairs of the brownstone she prayed that no one she knew from the theater would see her. D. W. Griffith, an imaginative, inventive filmmaker, was the director of the company. He was introducing delicate, young women on the screen because he knew the world loved youth. Mary at seventeen was just the right age. He thought she had lovely "golden curls," but—according to Mary—told her, "You're too little and too fat." Yet later he recalled, "The thing that most attracted me the day I first saw her was the intelligence that shone in her face." He hired Mary on a trial basis for five dollars a day for three days a week. She demanded a guarantee of twenty-five dollars a week and extra for overtime. Amused by her nerve, Griffith agreed.

For the screen test she chose a dress from the "wardrobe," a steel rack in the basement with clothes hanging on it. Most actors wore their own clothes in a film, but Biograph also supplied garments purchased from secondhand stores. The dresses were fumigated to kill lice, and Mary never forgot the bad smell.

The studio was located in the ballroom. Griffith told Mary her role in the story, and she improvised along with the other actors. The huge, three-hundred-pound camera was mounted on a platform and, when it started rolling, it made a deafening noise startling Mary. Later that day as she left the studio, she knew her performance had been "distinctly bad." Yet Griffith paid her, hired her full time, and even gave her a raise of ten dollars.

After her first day at Biograph, Griffith offered her a leading part. Mary was thrilled until he told her the role would require a love scene. She had never dated or kissed a boy. "I made up my mind right then and there that there would be no kissing," she wrote. Griffith called over a young actor, Owen Moore, and asked Mary to rehearse embracing him. The next day she did the scene and fell in love with Moore. But from then on, the director teasingly called her the "Great Unkissed."

As she made movies with Griffith, he urged her to naturally feel the parts, and to approach the camera simply and directly. For Griffith "the movie camera photographs an actor thinking." Later she revealed, "I learned more about acting under Griffith's guidance than I did in all my years in the theater."

Mary's curiosity drove her to learn everything about this new medium. "She was thirsty for work and information," recalled Griffith. Mary asked questions and studied lighting, costumes, editing, and camerawork. She was the cameraman's favorite because she understood his importance and tried different makeups to see what would photograph best in black and white. "There is something to me so sacred about that camera," she said.

Director D. W. Griffith holds a megaphone to shout commands. Cinematographers Karl Brown and Billy Blitzer are behind him during a production in 1916.

Strong-willed Mary often clashed with Griffith. When he wanted her to be more childlike on film, he demonstrated by doing what was described as running around "like a goose with its head off." Mary refused to imitate him. But they respected each other.

Over the next two and a half years, she made 103 movies with Griffith. The films were ten to twenty minutes long. He brought out her marvelous flair for comedy.

In those days, the actors' names were not usually displayed on the screen or released to the press. However, the *New York Dramatic Mirror* singled Mary out by reporting that it was on a "delicious" half-reel comedy (*They Would Elope*, 1909), featuring "an ingénue whose work in Biograph pictures is attracting attention."

After appearing in the 1910 film *Wilful Peggy*, three fans recognized her on the street. Mary immediately asked Griffith for a five-dollar raise. He had been trying to keep her from realizing her value because he was afraid that she would insist on a bigger salary. He also ordered all the fan mail addressed to "the girl with the golden curls" torn up before she could see it. But she knew the worth of her growing fame and stuck to her goal of supporting her family.

Sometimes Griffith cast Mary as a child, but she captured most hearts as a spirited teenager or newlywed. Off-screen, she hid her romance with actor Owen Moore because her mother disapproved of him. Five years older than Mary, Moore was known to be an alcoholic. When he left Griffith to work at the Independent Motion Picture Company (IMP), Pickford joined him. IMP was one of many independent film companies in those early days.

On January 7, 1911, she secretly married Moore. Mary was not yet nineteen and panicked. Overwhelmed with guilt, she slept at home that night.

When she finally told her family about the marriage, they were heartbroken. That summer of 1911, Mary left IMP and signed with a new company. She hammered out her contract, insisting that Moore would act and direct, but he had no talent and was jealous of her. Soon they separated, and Mary returned to Griffith.

Mary was now gaining a following and became known to audiences as "Little Mary." Her friends Lillian and Dorothy Gish, who were living in St. Louis, recognized her in one of her films. When they returned to New York, they went to Biograph and asked for Gladys Smith and discovered that she was Mary Pickford. When Mary introduced the Gish sisters to Griffith, he was taken with their beauty and hired them. The three young women competed for roles, but they always remained good friends.

Despite her growing success, Mary still yearned for the theater, so when Belasco offered her a part in the Broadway play *A Good Little Devil,* she took it. Finally, in 1913, she had the star's dressing room! Fans waited for her at the stage door because they knew her from her films.

The successful play became a successful movie in 1914. It was a fifty-minute film, becoming Mary's first feature-length movie. At last she received a screen credit from Famous Players—an independent studio: "Mary Pickford in *Tess of the Storm Country.*" She played a poor but feisty daughter of a fisherman. In one scene, when she's cornered by a villain three times her size, she grabs a flounder from her fish basket and clobbers him. In another scene, her neighbor cleans her up by washing her hair in a tub of suds. Audiences went crazy over the film. They adored Mary and loved her curls. "That was really the beginning of my career," she said. What had started as a demeaning way to earn money had come to be her passion.

Overnight, Mary became a huge movie star. People paid to see *her*, not the film. Movie magazines featured her photo. Her picture was printed on postcards and slipped into boxes of chocolates. She signed photos for her fans. And she wrote for a syndicated newspaper called *Daily Talks* that was actually written by her friend, screenwriter Frances Marion.

People considered her their personal friend. Mary had a gift for projecting on-screen the kind of person everyone wanted to meet and love. When asked why she had this hold on audiences she said, "It must be because I love them. I always have. I just had to have people's love."

With her incredible rise to fame and sharp business sense, and her mother Charlotte at her side, she negotiated a contract with Adolph Zukor's Famous Players for $1,000 a week (a typical year's earnings for a teacher or farmer) plus half the profits of her films. Soon she upped her salary to a million dollars a year for two years. At the age of twenty-four, Mary was the highest paid star in Hollywood.

She chose her own directors and cameramen to ensure the quality of her films, experimenting as she went along and supervising every detail of production, down to the advertising. She also selected her scripts.

In *The Poor Little Rich Girl*, which her friend Frances Marion adapted from a stage play, Mary portrayed a child throughout the film. At five feet, she was physically small, and the art director made her appear even shorter by designing oversize furniture. In an article for *Vogue*, she explained her technique for acting childlike: opening her eyes wide in surprise, pouting when displeased, and pointing her toes inward. She said, "I am living the childhood that was denied me when I was a little girl myself."

Although she could afford to buy the lovely clothes she had admired as a child actor on tour, Pickford had to wear prim dresses with lace collars to maintain her wholesome image off-screen. And she lived simply, commuting between homes in California and New York. (The movie industry had gone west to take advantage of the steady sunlight and variety of locations.)

At a party in 1916, she met actor Douglas Fairbanks, famed for his swashbuckling roles and daredevil stunts. They met again at a dance and fell in love. She was still legally married to Owen Moore, and Fairbanks was married, too. They kept their romance a secret for fear of upsetting their publics.

But soon more important events took place. In spring 1917, the United States declared war against Germany and entered World War I. Mary made patriotic movies to encourage men to enlist. With Fairbanks and his best friend, comedy actor Charlie Chaplin, she raised millions of dollars for Liberty Bonds to help pay for the war effort. In Chicago she even auctioned one of her precious curls for $15,000!

After the war ended in 1918, Mary, Fairbanks, and Chaplin thought about forming their own film distribution company. Why share their profits? They could distribute the films themselves and have complete creative control. In 1919, they met with D. W. Griffith and actor William S. Hart, the cowboy star of silent Westerns.

The Founders of United Artists. From left: Douglas Fairbanks, Mary Pickford, Charlie Chaplin, and D. W. Griffith, 1919.

Together they established United Artists Corporation (UA). UA had no actual studio lot but distributed the films made by independent producers. Before the final documents were signed, Hart withdrew and the four partners at UA made their own films on their own lots —using UA as their distributor. Mary's first UA film (in 1920) was *Pollyanna,* adapted by Frances Marion from the children's classic, then a remake of *Tess of the Storm Country* (1922), and a string of hits—some based on children's books such as *Little Lord Fauntleroy* (1921) and *Little Annie Rooney* (1925).

Mary Pickford in a tense scene from *Tess of the Storm Country*, 1922

Mary's romance with Fairbanks deepened, and they obtained divorces from their spouses. She worried that her fans would not forgive her when she married Fairbanks on March 28, 1920. Stopping in New York on their way to Europe for a honeymoon, cheering crowds greeted them. Because of their wide appeal, admirers mobbed them everywhere they went.

Douglas Fairbanks does a handstand as Mary Pickford is about to take his picture on the roof of a New York hotel, 1920.

Back in Beverly Hills, they lived in a grand house and were considered Hollywood royalty. They acted in and produced movies side-by-side at their ten-acre Pickford-Fairbanks Studio. Many of the independent producers owned their own properties. European directors were invited to visit the Pickford-Fairbanks Studio and make pictures. By 1926, filmmaking was the largest industry in Los Angeles.

Mary, her husband, and more than thirty leaders in the film business formed the Academy of Motion Picture Arts and Sciences in 1927. Mary was one of three women. One of the Academy's goals was to educate fans about the art of film and to honor performances with annual awards. These came to be known as the Academy Awards. Mary and Fairbanks also set up the first film school at the University of Southern California.

In 1927, Mary made her last silent film, a romantic comedy, *My Best Girl*. She played a salesgirl in a department store who has a romance with the owner's son, played by a handsome young actor, Buddy Rogers.

Throughout her career, Mary stayed close to her mother, who helped her negotiate contracts and often traveled with her. In 1925, Charlotte had become ill with breast cancer and refused to have surgery. Her condition worsened, and Mary took her to her beach house to rest. On March 21, 1928, Charlotte died. Mary said she never recovered from her mother's death. Three months later, she cut off her trademark curls for the role in *Coquette*. The style for women then was short, bobbed hair, and Mary had resisted because her mother adored her the way she was. The haircut made the front page of the *New York Times*: "Mary Pickford Secretly

Buddy Rogers had a crush on Mary Pickford as they
playfully charmed audiences in *My Best Girl*, 1927.

Has Her Curls Shorn; Forsakes Little-Girl Roles to be 'Grown Up.'"
Fans were shocked. But Mary said of her curls, "They're gone and
I'm glad. I couldn't go on being Rebecca and Tess and Pollyanna . . .
forever." Now in her midthirties, she wanted to act her age in films.

Mary showed off her hairdo in her first talkie, *Coquette*, in
1929. The introduction of talking pictures in 1927 had sent waves of
panic through Hollywood. Mary had thought it was a passing fad
but soon realized that silent films were finished. Many performers'
careers ended because their voices sounded ridiculous.

She felt confident about her voice because of her theater
experience. But *Coquette* experienced technical problems that
made the sound tinny. Even Mary wasn't sure of the right way to talk

in films. She seemed stiff as she played a wealthy young Southern woman, and her performance lacked the spirit she had shown as Tess. Nevertheless, she won the second Academy Award (later called the Oscar) in 1930 for Best Actress, and more than forty years later (in 1976) received an Honorary Oscar for "her unique contributions to the film industry."

The 1930s were a tough time for the film industry. The Great Depression hit the country. Millions of Americans lost their jobs and couldn't afford food and housing, much less movie tickets. Film attendance dropped. Mary made a few talkies but knew the films were not up to the standard of her best work in silents. She believed that her early movies would seem old-fashioned to modern audiences and they would laugh at her. In 1933 she retired, tossed her films into storage, and considered burning them. Her friends were outraged. "They don't belong to you," insisted Lillian Gish. "They belong to the public."

She knew they were right and came to recognize the importance of her films as the beginning of an American art form. To celebrate, she hosted a party in 1935 for the head of the new film department at New York's Museum of Modern Art. They agreed that the silent films were "the only great art" of the twentieth century and that Mary represented that art. In 1945, she donated some negatives to MoMA and others to the Library of Congress.

Film historians pay tribute to Mary for inventing screen acting. But she once said, "I didn't act—I *was* the characters I played on the screen. During a picture, I didn't leave the character at the studio; I took it home with me. I lived my parts."

A gun pokes through the wall terrifying Dorothy Gish as her sister Lillian Gish cowers in a corner in *An Unseen Enemy*, 1912.

CHAPTER 2 LILLIAN GISH

"GRIFFITH ALWAYS TOLD US THERE WAS NO QUICK OR EASY WAY TO STARDOM. YOU WERE A STAR ONLY WHEN YOU HAD WON YOUR WAY INTO THE HEARTS OF PEOPLE."
—Lillian Gish

When they met D. W. Griffith at Biograph Studios, Lillian and Dorothy Gish were sitting huddled on a bench. The sight of them enchanted Griffith. "Of the two," he said, "Lillian shone with an exquisitely fragile ethereal beauty." She was nineteen but pretended to be sixteen. Dorothy was fourteen. The sisters were in awe of Griffith.

"He was imposing," remembered Lillian. "He held himself like a king."

Griffith whisked them up to the rehearsal hall to see if they could act. Since the sisters looked alike, he gave Lillian a blue bow for her hair, and Dorothy a red ribbon so that he could tell them apart. He told them the story they were about to perform: two girls are trapped in a house while thieves try to break in and rob the safe. There was no script. Griffith had made up the story and called out directions: "Red, you hear a strange noise. . . . Blue, you're scared too." Although the sisters were really terrified, they didn't show enough emotion. "Tell the camera what you feel," ordered Griffith. "Look scared."

"It was not difficult," recalled Lillian. "We were already practically paralyzed with fright."

"No, that's not enough!" shouted Griffith. Suddenly he pulled out a gun and chased them around the room firing shots. Lillian thought he had gone crazy and didn't realize he was shooting at the ceiling. Finally, he put away his gun and said, "That will make a wonderful scene." He invited them to return the next day and film the movie they had just rehearsed. They did, and *An Unseen Enemy*, released in 1912, was their first movie. Their friend Mary Pickford, who had sent them to Griffith, scolded him for his rude manners. From then on, he called the Gish sisters Miss Lillian and Miss Dorothy. But Lillian was not enthusiastic about making movies. "Wordless acting" seemed "weird," she wrote to her best friend in Ohio. She wasn't even sure about her future in the movies.

The sisters started earning a living as stage actors when they were children. Lillian was born in Springfield, Ohio, on October 14, 1893, and Dorothy was born on March 11, 1898, in Dayton, Ohio. Their mother, Mary, whom they adored, was an actress in stock companies that traveled from place to place to perform plays. Their father had "disappeared" from their lives, and they hardly ever heard from him. Lillian later said, "Insecurity was a great gift. I think it taught me to work as if everything depended on me."

Sometimes she toured with "Aunt" Alice, a family friend, while her mother and sister worked with another company. Best of all was when the family was together. Although the girls did not attend school regularly, their mother always carried a history book. "We had our lessons in dressing rooms, stations, rented rooms," recalled Lillian. "Dorothy and I loved it."

During the summer, before the theater season began, they stayed with relatives in Massillon, Ohio. In the autumn, they went to New York agencies to find parts. "The problem of money was always with us," wrote Lillian. So when Mary suggested doing movies between stage jobs, they auditioned for Griffith. Meanwhile, they heard that Broadway producer David Belasco needed young actresses for his play *A Good Little Devil*. He had cast Mary Pickford as the lead and hired Lillian to be the Golden Fairy. Although it was "a very small part," wrote Lillian to her friend, the theater was the real place for an actress, and she planned "to do pictures on the side."

That summer of 1912 Lillian also appeared in a few movies for Griffith. In the fall she told him that she had to leave to start rehearsing *A Good Little Devil,* and he offered to pay her fifty dollars if she became a permanent member of his company. Griffith said his offer would stand if she ever wanted to accept it. Lillian, excited to be in the play, stayed in New York while Dorothy went to California with Griffith and his crew. Their mother went to Ohio to work in a candy shop.

Lillian's role as the Golden Fairy required flying, and she was suspended above the stage with wire straps. During a performance in Baltimore the wires came loose, and she fell off a five-foot wall. The audience laughed. She wasn't hurt but felt humiliated and lonely, so she came up with a plan. When the play opened in New York, she pretended to be sick—and it worked! Belasco sent her to California to join her sister. Her mother left Ohio to take care of her.

Although moviemaking had started on the East Coast, independent companies relocated to Los Angeles during the winter months. Cameras at the time needed bright sunlight to capture images. Biograph Studios was an open-air stage consisting of a wooden floor built on the site of an old streetcar barn. Casting was not decided until just before filming, so everyone in the company had to rehearse each part. One day Lillian might play the lead, and the next day a small part. Griffith discouraged vanity among his actors and didn't want them to receive fan mail, so he instructed his workers to tear up any—as he had done with Mary Pickford. "The films were important, not the players," recalled Lillian.

Film itself was expensive, so a scene was shot only once. Griffith sat on a high kitchen chair calling out the plot. "Don't act it, feel it," he commanded. Lillian learned a new kind of acting and began to enjoy this method of telling stories. She showed her emotions by the way she walked and ran, and she overcame her shyness when the camera moved in for a close-up of her face. It was her job to "make the character believable to an audience." They rehearsed for days, sometimes weeks. "Everything was planned and timed," said Lillian. Soon she lost all her "snobbishness" about performing in movies and wrote to a friend, telling her which films to see that included the Gish sisters.

In 1913, Lillian won the lead in *The Mothering Heart*, a melodramatic twenty-nine-minute two-reeler. Although Lillian was twenty (and claiming to be seventeen), she gave a moving performance as a married woman that showcased her talent for tragedy. Her frail beauty and suffering on-screen touched audiences. Lillian not only cared about her acting, but all aspects of filmmaking. She went to the darkroom to review her rushes (the unedited footage of the film). She watched the printing of the negatives to make sure they caught the mood the actors were trying to get. Griffith trusted her judgment.

When the company returned to New York, rumor spread that

Griffith was leaving Biograph, and Lillian and Dorothy hoped he would take them wherever he was going. Lillian said that Griffith was like a father to her, and she felt loyal to him. He sparked her imagination, and she was thrilled to be part of "the creation of a new art form."

In October 1913, Griffith teamed up with producers Harry and Roy Aitken to head their company, Mutual Productions. Lillian and Dorothy left Biograph to work with him on *The Rebellion of Kitty Belle*, which was released in 1914. Without Griffith's permission, Mutual released photos of Lillian and Dorothy with the caption: "Two Famous Sisters." Griffith disapproved. He told Lillian that she wouldn't be a famous star until she had "won her way into the hearts of people" and her name became "a household word." That would take thirty years. Lillian doubted that she would ever become a star.

But for his next film, *The Birth of a Nation* (1915), Griffith allowed the actors' names to appear on the program for the first time. The film was based on a book, *The Clansman* by Thomas Dixon, Jr. The novel depicted Black people unfairly, romanticized slavery, and presented the Ku Klux Klan as heroes. Griffith, a native of Kentucky, intended to use the story to tell his version of the Civil War.

Lillian didn't expect a major part, but Griffith tried her out as Elsie Stoneman, the romantic heroine from the North, and she won the role. She prepared for the film by studying *Godey's Lady's Book,* which showed clothes and hairstyles of the period, and photographs of the Civil War. Her costumes were specially made, and it was her job to remember what she had worn in each scene,

Hartsook Photo took this head-and-shoulders portrait of Lillian Gish on January 1, 1915.

Henry Walthall as Colonel Ben Cameron kisses the hand of Lillian Gish playing Elsie Stoneman in *The Birth of a Nation*, 1915.

and how her hair and makeup looked. "We had to rehearse how to sit and how to move in the hoop skirts of the day," she wrote. Shooting started at 5:00 a.m. to make the most of the sunlight. Griffith directed the battle scenes like a general, shouting orders through a megaphone. The first part depicted the war, the second part, the chaos of Reconstruction.

The movie premiered on February 8, 1915, in Los Angeles, and ran for two hours and forty-five minutes. Lillian sat at the end of a row of men and said, "During parts of it [the film] the whole row shook with sobs. It was so moving."

However, *The Birth of a Nation* drew angry criticism from leaders in the African American community. The National Association for the Advancement of Colored People (NAACP), which had been founded in 1909 to protest violence against African Americans and promote equal rights, tried to block the New York opening. The organization charged in court that the movie was a threat to public safety. Donald Bogle, a Black film historian wrote, "*The Birth of a Nation* gave birth to the shocking and degrading stereotypes that were to plague African American movie images throughout the twentieth century."

When Lillian had viewed the first run-through of the complete film she praised Griffith and expressed gratitude for having been part of the movie. Perhaps blinded by her admiration of his work, and her devotion to him, she defended the film. Critic James Agee later hailed the movie as "the birth of an art." Nevertheless, critics still attack the film's racism even though they celebrate Griffith's pioneering camera techniques.

Dorothy didn't appear in *The Birth of a Nation,* but she was featured in a series of comedies. Griffith used both sisters in a later movie, *Hearts of the World.* World War I had broken out in Europe in 1914, and the prime minister of England asked Griffith to make a film that would bring America into the conflict as an ally of England and France. Griffith agreed. By the time the United States entered the war in 1917, Griffith was already in London preparing *Hearts of the World.*

He sent for Lillian and Dorothy to star in the movie, and they sailed to England with their mother. The story told of the effect of war on civilians in a French village. Shortly after the filmmakers arrived, Germans bombed London in the first daytime air raids and bombing continued, day and night. "Have been through three raids now," Lillian wrote to her friend. "The last one at midnight was the most terrible thing I hope I will ever have to go through. . . . We could hear the cries in our rooms of the wounded and dying." Later they stood before a shattered school building and wept at the wreckage where sixteen children had been killed. Lillian's firsthand experience of war deeply pained her and inspired her heartfelt performance.

After six months of work, they sailed home, and completed the movie in Hollywood. *Hearts of the World* premiered on March 12, 1918, and successfully raised thousands of dollars for the war effort. Dorothy's outstanding portrayal of a street singer led to a million-dollar offer from Paramount Studios, but she turned down the offer, preferring to stay with Griffith.

Lillian was now Griffith's leading lady and considered the greatest American actress on the screen. Her weekly salary jumped to $1,500, then $1,850. She, her sister, and mother rented a spacious house in Los Angeles with a tennis court and rose garden.

In the fall of 1918, Griffith discussed a new film idea with Lillian about a brutal prizefighter who beats his twelve-year-old daughter, and a Chinese poet who tries to help the girl. Lillian objected to playing the daughter because she was now twenty-five. But Griffith insisted that a young girl couldn't possibly do the final tragic scenes and told her to find some clothes in wardrobe for the part.

That day Lillian didn't feel well. After her dress fitting, she started to walk home, and was so weak and dizzy, that she had to stop and lie down under bushes to rest before going on. By the time she reached her house she crawled up the stairs and collapsed on her bed. Her temperature was 106! The doctor arrived and said that Lillian had Spanish flu. The pandemic was sweeping the country and infecting people worldwide. Some victims died within a few days. There was no cure, and Lillian's family was terrified. She wasn't frightened, though. "I was too sick to care," she recalled.

On the morning of November 18, her fever broke. She heard bells ringing and thought she was delirious, but her mother told her that the war was over. Lillian quickly recovered. Wearing a gauze medical mask, she returned to work on the new movie and kept her mask on when she was off camera. Griffith, afraid of catching the virus, stayed ten feet away from her. The film, *Broken Blossoms*, was released in May by United Artists, the independent company that Griffith had *just* formed with Mary Pickford, Douglas Fairbanks, and Charlie Chaplin. The *New York Times* praised it as "a masterpiece in moving pictures." Lillian said, "It was the best part I ever had and my favorite picture."

In the fall of 1919, Griffith moved his company to Mamaroneck, New York, and Lillian followed with her family. When he asked Lillian to direct her sister in a movie, she was "dumbfounded."

But he said, "You know as much as I do about making pictures." She and Dorothy wrote the script titled *Remodeling Her Husband*, a story about a wife, played by Dorothy, whose husband complains that no one ever notices her. She tricks him by having him follow her down the street as she makes funny faces at every man who passes her. Of course, each one turns around to look at her. Actor James Rennie took the part of the husband, and he and Dorothy fell in love on the set. Rehearsals of their romantic scenes lasted too long, and Lillian shouted "unhug" through her megaphone. When she finished directing, cutting, and editing the picture, she felt relieved. "Would never do it again," she wrote to her friend. "I am not strong enough. I doubt if any woman is." An odd comment since the entire crew was female.

The following year, Lillian made one of her last movies with Griffith, *Way Down East*. She played the ultimate "helpless heroine," a woman who has been betrayed by a scoundrel and is thrown out of a cabin by her employer during a blizzard. She stumbles through the snow toward a raging river. Collapses on an ice floe. Floats downstream toward a waterfall, her hair trailing in the icy water. Griffith insisted on filming in a real blizzard and waited with the cast and crew in Vermont. The storm struck in March, and as they filmed, Lillian's face was caked with ice and snow. Icicles formed on her eyelashes. "*Get that face!*" Griffith shouted to the cameraman. In the final moments, the hero wades through the frigid water to rescue Lillian. They repeated the sequence with Lillian on a slab of ice twenty times a day for three weeks. In later years she said, "This kind of dedication probably seems foolish today, but it wasn't unusual then. No sacrifice was too great to get the film right, to get it accurate, true, and perfect." The movie opened in September 1920 and was a hit. A critic later wrote, "Lillian Gish's acting in this film was perhaps her very best for Griffith."

That year was the same year Dorothy and James eloped to Greenwich, Connecticut, after shooting a movie. But Dorothy didn't want to leave home, and she and James moved in with her mother and sister.

Lillian Gish, the helpless heroine, wanders on the ice in *Way Down East*, 1920 *(above)*. Lillian Gish collapsed on an ice floe in *Way Down East (below)*.

Lillian did one more movie with Griffith, *Orphans of the Storm*, a story about Henriette (Lillian) and her adopted sister Louise (Dorothy) who goes blind. This was one of the few times Lillian and Dorothy acted *as sisters* in a film. Viewers felt their love as they hugged and kissed again and again throughout the movie. Griffith set the film in the period of the French Revolution. Lillian designed her own costumes based on research with history professors and experts on the period. *Orphans* opened in December of 1921 and President Warren Harding invited the sisters and Griffith to the White House for lunch and a private screening.

After twenty years with Griffith, Lillian Gish was an established star. Griffith said, "I can't afford to pay you what you're worth. You should go out on your own." He knew she could earn a higher salary with one of the other studios because she had box office power, but she was frightened at the prospect of leaving him. "I began to wonder whether I'd ever be able to act under another director," she wrote, "whether, in truth, I was an actress at all." But critics and audiences thought Griffith needed Lillian more than she needed him. Her greatest films that followed were *The Scarlet Letter* (1926) and *The Wind* (1928).

Movie magazines portrayed her as "the perfect girl"—old fashion, modest, "a *very* serious actress." Lillian received three to four hundred fan letters a week. In 1924, she signed with MGM to do six pictures for one million dollars, while Dorothy went to Paramount Studios. They both easily transitioned to talkies. Lillian had always expected to return to the theater someday, and she did in 1930. From then on, she performed steadily onstage while occasionally acting in movies. She appeared in front of the camera

Lillian Gish as Henriette comforts her adopted blind sister Louise played by Dorothy Gish in *Orphans of the Storm*, 1921.

for a total of seventy-five years and won dozens of honors and tributes.

Lillian lectured on the history of movies and wrote about the "universal language" of silents that spoke to all people. "The faces and eyes are better than the words," she explained. She donated her early movies to the Film Library at the Museum of Modern Art (MoMA) in New York. She also formed the Gish Foundation, which gave money to the Library of Congress and the New York Public Library of Performing Arts to preserve and exhibit films, and spoke at silent film festivals. In 1971, she received an Honorary Oscar for her contribution to motion pictures.

Upon receiving her award Lillian said, "It was our privilege to serve that beautiful thing, the film. And we never doubted for a moment that it was the most powerful thing, the mind and heartbeat of our technical century."

Portrait of Frances Marion, 1915

CHAPTER 3 FRANCES MARION

"I OWE MY GREATEST SUCCESS TO WOMEN."   —Frances Marion

For more than twenty years, Frances Marion was the highest paid screenwriter—male or female—in Hollywood. Her story reads like a movie. Bright, beautiful, and energetic, Marion wrote many of her friend Mary Pickford's biggest successes.

Yet she started out wanting to be an artist. Marion Benson Owens was born in San Francisco to a wealthy family on November 18, 1888. She attended an exclusive boarding school and was not only good at art, but also excelled in writing. Her poem "California's Latest," about a new kind of daisy, was published in *Sunset Magazine*'s May 1905 issue with her own illustrations. At age sixteen, she enrolled in art school and had a tremendous crush on her instructor. But the disastrous San Francisco earthquake of 1906 and fires that followed changed everything. Marion's father's drug company and warehouses were destroyed, and so was the art school. Only the family's house remained standing. Her parents couldn't afford to send her to college, so she married her instructor before her eighteenth birthday.

The marriage didn't last, and Marion looked for work to support herself. Using the short stories she had written at school as writing samples, she landed a job as a cub reporter for the *San Francisco Examiner*. Her boss sent her to cover the opening of a show starring vaudeville comedian Marie Dressler. Backstage, Dressler refused to see anyone, but Marion called out, "If I don't get this

45

interview, I'll lose my job." The actress sympathized and talked with her while Marion sketched and wrote. This kindness marked a turning point in Marion's life, leading to the Hollywood film business in a roundabout way.

A second marriage brought her to Los Angeles, and she worked painting posters of actors for a theater producer. One day she bumped into Marie Dressler who remembered her. Dressler was in town filming *Tillie's Punctured Romance* (1914), the first feature-length comedy (with a running time of 1 hour and 23 minutes). Her stories about making movies enthralled Marion, and Dressler suggested that she consider working as an actress. "You've got the looks," she said. Marion wanted to be more than a pretty ingenue, but she accepted Dressler's invitation to visit her on the set. When she arrived, she learned that Dressler had finished shooting and had left, but Marion felt excited just standing at the studio gates. "The movie bug had stung me," she wrote. "I sensed a future in this fascinating if cockeyed business." How could she get started? Despite all the accolades for her beauty, she wanted to use her mind.

It was a stroke of luck that the theater producer let her go because he couldn't afford to print posters. Out of work, Marion tracked down her friend Adela Rogers St. Johns, a young journalist she knew from San Francisco. "Were the movies a passing fad or here to stay?" she asked Adela. "They are here to stay," said Adela, and introduced Marion to people in the film business. Marion met actor Owen Moore. He had seen her posters and arranged for her to make a portrait of his movie star wife Mary Pickford.

Marion struck up a friendship with Mary. They were both smart, pretty, and fiercely ambitious. Marion didn't do a portrait of Mary as planned, but afterward she felt determined to find a job in "the movies."

Nothing immediately came of her meeting with Mary, so Marion hit on another idea. Through Adela, she met Lois Weber, one of the best-known women directors and scriptwriters in Los Angeles. Lois and her husband produced feature films. Marion showed Lois her drawings, hoping to design costumes and sets. But once again it was her looks that made an impression. Lois said, "Would you like to come under my wing as one of my little starlets?"

Husband and wife, and codirectors Phillips Smalley and Lois Weber review a script, undated.

Marion told her that she didn't want to be an actress, but Lois explained that at her studio, everybody did a little bit of everything. "How soon can you start?" she asked. Marion realized this was her chance. Two hours later, she signed a contract with the studio that listed her as an actress with a new Hollywood name, Frances Marion.

As Lois's assistant, she did everything from writing press releases and painting backgrounds, to cutting film. She loved learning about moviemaking but wasn't sure where she fit in. Lois noted Marion's intelligence and asked her to write dialogue for the extras. Audiences were beginning to read the lips of the actors who had conversations during filming that had nothing to do with the story. Marion wrote lines for them and acted with them in costume to make sure they spoke the correct words. Her career as a scenario writer began, a line here and a line there.

Women writers were commonplace in the film industry then. Scenario writing—sometimes a short synopsis of a story—was talked up as "a new profession for women." When Lois and her husband left to go to Universal, Marion accepted a writing position at another studio, but it didn't work out. Neither did her marriage, and she and her husband divorced.

Through Hollywood gossip, Mary Pickford heard that Marion was unhappy and offered her a job. Although it involved acting, Mary assured her that she could also write scenarios and they'd "have fun together." They did, costarring in *A Girl of Yesterday* (1915). After shooting each day, Marion developed her own script for *The Foundling*, a story about a twelve-year-old orphan. Marion's art training enabled her to imagine the action and fantasy sequences of silent films and describe the images in words for the

Mary Pickford on the left and Frances Marion on the right, about 1918

actors and director to follow. "This started a whole new school of movie writing," wrote Adela. Mary liked the script, showed it to the head of the studio, and he bought it for $125. Marion said, "I ceased walking on this earth."

The Foundling was shot in New York, and Marion rode the train cross-country for the opening. When she arrived, Mary told her the terrible news that the negative of *The Foundling* had burned in a laboratory fire. Marion was bitterly disappointed. She was counting on the movie's success to lead to a writing contract. Although the script was safe, reshooting the film had to be postponed to fit Mary's busy schedule.

Bent on achieving her goal, Marion wrote to producers and proposed working for two weeks without pay to prove her ability as a screenwriter. William Brady at World Films agreed. At his studio in Fort Lee, New Jersey, Marion sat down at her desk, faced her typewriter, and had no ideas. Then she remembered a lesson Lois had taught her: "A good editor can make even a mediocre film seem important." Marion viewed five World Films that had never been released because they were so bad and laughed out loud at the worst of them. She transformed the awful melodrama into

Frances Marion types a script at her desk, undated.

a comedy by inventing opening and closing scenes. Brady read Marion's revisions, shot the new scenes, and the movie was a winner. He hired her for $200 a week, a record-breaking sum for that time.

Her friend, Mary, who had become the highest-ranking star in Hollywood, insisted that Marion write her next film. Marion adapted the play *The Poor Little Rich Girl* (1917). Mary, in her midtwenties, performed as an unhappy preteen imprisoned in a mansion with unloving parents and mean servants. She and Marion mischievously added bits of slapstick. When studio executives watched the film, they hated it and didn't want to release it. But the film had already been booked into theaters all over the country, so it had to be shown. Marion agonized, sure that she had wrecked her best friend's career. Yet Mary insisted that they attend the opening. To their amazement, the packed house laughed in all the right places and sniffled and sobbed during the sad moments. At the end, "Applause sounded like thunder," remembered Marion. Pickford hugged her and exclaimed, "It's a hit!"

They had learned a good lesson. "Although we respected the opinion of the bosses," wrote Marion, "we realized that a comedy never should be shown without an audience." From then on, Mary's films were previewed in neighborhood theaters, a practice that became an industry standard.

Marion signed a contract with Adolph Zukor's Famous Players Studio, one of several small companies, to write "special features for Mary Pickford." Now they were a team. Books gave Marion ideas for screenplays, but she found that she could only use a third of a book. "The screen version must move at a faster pace," she said.

Mary Pickford (left) as the boisterous Rebecca of
Sunnybrook Farm in a movie adapted by Frances Marion
from the book of the same name, 1917.

"It is absolutely necessary to have action in our screen stories."

From 1915 to 1917, they produced silent classics such as *A Little Princess*. Marion's sixty-page script included stage directions, camera angles, and title cards. Due to her growing fame with Mary, other studios hired her as well, and she earned more than any other screenwriter.

Beyond Hollywood, the world was changing. In April 1917, the United States declared war on Germany and entered World War I. Studio heads cooperated with the government to produce patriotic movies. Marion wanted to do her part by going overseas as a war correspondent. She asked her friend, Mary Roberts Rinehart, a writer who had just returned from covering the European war, to help her get an assignment. Rinehart agreed if Marion would write a film to inspire enlistment. So Marion wrote *Johanna Enlists* (1918) for Mary Pickford. They visited the 143rd Field Artillery based at Camp Kearney, near San Diego, to discuss the regiment's appearing in the movie, and met with the chaplain, Fred Thomson. During filming, Fred and Marion fell in love and got engaged. That summer, before *Johanna Enlists*'s release, Marion gave up her huge salary and volunteered to make a documentary about the 20,000 American women serving in Europe.

On September 18, 1918, she sailed to France, and teamed up with Hollywood cameramen to film the work American women were doing for the soldiers. When asked if she could use any of her experiences for a scenario, Marion replied, "The awfulness of what I saw . . . was utterly beyond my powers of comprehension, let alone my ability to describe. . . . I could not write of the war, of the agonies, of the bravery of our boys, or the things they endured."

While she was still in Europe, the Allied powers—Great Britain, France, Italy, Japan, and the United States—signed an agreement with Germany to stop fighting. As the war ended, the international flu pandemic struck, and Marion was one of hundreds of thousands who caught the virus. Slowly she recovered, and in February 1919, returned to California.

Back home she received a telegram from William Randolph Hearst. The newspaper publisher had founded Cosmopolitan Pictures in New York, and he offered Marion a contract for $100,000 a year (over a million dollars today) to write scripts. Marion accepted on the condition that she could be loaned out to other studios. For ideas, she read stories in Hearst's *Cosmopolitan* magazine. *Humoresque* (1920), a saga of a Jewish mother's love and sacrifice for her son, particularly moved her. It did not appeal to Hearst, but Marion convinced him to make the movie. Audiences connected with the story, proving Marion's rule: "Give the audience characters with whom it can sympathize or at least like." *Photoplay* magazine ran a contest for fans to vote on the greatest picture of the year for 1920, and *Humoresque* won the magazine's Gold Medal of Honor.

Marion's fiancé had returned from serving in Europe, and they married. He and Marion settled in Los Angeles. Fred became interested in acting and with his athletic ability performed stunts in serials. But he really wanted to do realistic films about the West without gun violence, which he thought was harmful for kids in the audience. After training with his horse Silver King, he won contracts for feature films and became a cowboy star. Marion churned out scripts for him with plenty of action.

Lieutenant Frances Marion, a war correspondent, arrives in New York on the ocean liner *Baltic* from Germany, February 7, 1919.

Westerns grew in popularity as movies became big business. With over thirty filmmaking companies, Los Angeles was now the center of film production. Marion was constantly in demand, writing hundreds of pages in pencil on yellow pads each day, and using books for story lines. She was the undisputed "champion of successfully taking books to the screen."

In 1925, producer Irving Thalberg at MGM, hired her to make a silent movie version of the classic American novel *The Scarlet Letter* by Nathaniel Hawthorne. The book, set in the seventeenth century, begins with a crowd in front of the jail as Hester Prynne, a young woman holding a baby, comes out and is punished in public for having an illegitimate child. Marion wanted the audience to immediately feel sorry for Hester, so she opened the movie *before* Hester's punishment. The first pages of her script establish Hester's mood. The scenario reads, "We see a young woman alone with a spinning wheel in the corner as she prepares for church. She buttons herself into her dove grey dress . . ." Hester looks sad and lonely.

Lillian Gish starred as Hester, and Marion felt honored to work with her. The movie was a smash! It was one of Lillian's last great silents. Around this time, studio heads began debating the merits of talking pictures. Some producers thought it was a craze that would last for only a few months. However, Marion believed that sound pictures were inevitable. She was excited at the prospect of introducing real sounds for dramatic effect.

She was also thrilled about her personal life. Marion had become pregnant, and on December 8, 1926, gave birth to her son Fred, Jr. Sadly, her happy life ended weeks later, on Christmas Day of 1928. Marion's beloved husband died of a tetanus infection. Fred was thirty-eight. Marion was devastated, too miserable to work for months.

By the time she returned to MGM, where she was under contract, the studio had converted to talking pictures. Producers brought in "dialogue writers" from the theater to take charge of the scripts. "The results were not satisfactory," recalled Marion. The dialogue was terrible. Playwrights didn't understand pacing, and the movies they made were "dull, over talked, and overacted." The studio heads eventually left experienced scenarists like Marion to do their job.

She was comfortable writing words for her characters when their ideas and thoughts couldn't be conveyed just through action. Her choice of words revealed the speakers' personalities and backgrounds. To research *The Big House*, a 1930 crime drama set in a prison, she visited San Quentin, and watched and listened to the convicts. Marion introduced sound effects as part of the plot. The movie opens with the rumble of hundreds of prisoners stomping down a hall, and the audience sees only their legs and shoes. In another scene, the inmates protest the rotten food, and the clanging of one metal cup on the table builds to a deafening racket as all the convicts join in. The movie, an original story inspired by newspaper articles demanding prison reform, won Marion an Oscar for Best Writing Achievement. She was the first woman to win the award. In 1932, she received a second Oscar in the category Original Story later called Best Original Screenplay for *The Champ*, a love story about a drunken, down-and-out boxer and his adoring young son.

Marie Dressler shows off her comedic style in this 1916
photo taken at a New York City charity event.

With three hundred scripts to her credit—from dramas to comedies and Westerns—Marion wrote *How to Write and Sell Film Stories,* the first textbook on the subject. She invited students from the film school founded by Mary Pickford and Douglas Fairbanks at the University of Southern California, to come to her house for roundtable discussions. If she hadn't been given opportunities at the beginning, she wouldn't have learned.

Marion never forgot the women who had helped her. When she heard that her old friend Marie Dressler was sick and desperately poor, Marion was determined to do something for the first person who had given her a break. She knew that the only help Dressler would accept would be the chance to work. Marion developed a story that her studio, MGM, had already bought, invented slapstick gags that would fit Dressler's comic style, then persuaded her boss, Irving Thalberg, to hire the actress. Dressler was overjoyed. Working on the film restored her health and spirits as well as launched her comeback as a top box office star.

Throughout her long career, Marion remained loyal and loving to her friends. Marion and Mary Pickford sent each other flowers on birthdays and holidays, and in April 1965, celebrated the fifty years of their professional partnership. Marion wrote a memoir and an interviewer asked her what she wanted readers to take away from the book. Marion said, "I hope my story shows one thing—how many women gave me real aid when I stood at the crossroads. . . .

"I owe my greatest success to women."

Autographed portrait of Louise Beavers, undated

CHAPTER 4

LOUISE BEAVERS

"I AM ONLY PLAYING THE PARTS. I DON'T LIVE THEM."

—Louise Beavers

L ouise Beavers was one of the first and best-known Black
   actresses who worked in Hollywood. But some film critics and
   historians have forgotten her, although she appeared in more
than 200 movies that showcased her talent.

Born on March 8, 1902, in Cincinnati, Ohio, she and her parents
moved to Pasadena, California, when she was eleven because
her mother, a schoolteacher, had health problems. In this warmer
climate, Louise's mother worked as a voice teacher and trained
her daughter for the concert stage. Louise sang in the local church
choir, and after graduating from Pasadena High School in 1920, she
joined the Lady Minstrels, a group of young women who performed
at amateur productions.

Stories vary as to how she got started in the movies. According
to one source, Louise displayed her talent when she performed with
the Lady Minstrels at a theater in downtown Los Angeles. Movie
historian Donald Bogle wrote that she "perfected the optimistic,
sentimental black woman whose sweet, sunny disposition and kind-
heartedness almost always saved the day." Executives from Universal
Studios called Louise three times before she responded to their
offers for an audition. She resisted because of "the African roles given
to colored people." Louise said, "In all the pictures I had seen . . . they
never used colored people for anything except savages."

Others say that her break came at age eighteen when she took a job as a personal maid and assistant to silent film star Leatrice Joy. Joy was at the top of her career then, appearing in films directed by Cecil B. DeMille. Louise worked for her for twelve years and occasionally performed in movies as a walk-on or extra.

Yet according to *Negro Digest*, Louise was discovered when she sang "Pal of My Old Cradle Days" in an amateur contest at the Philharmonic Auditorium in Los Angeles. "I didn't know how good I was," she said. A few days later she received a call from an agent at the Central Casting Bureau who recruited Black actors to appear in Hollywood films. She auditioned and won the part of "slave at wedding" in *Uncle Tom's Cabin*, a 1927 silent film, launching her acting career.

From then on, Louise worked steadily in movies, playing minor roles as maids, housekeepers, and mammies. These stereotypical types were the only parts offered to Black actresses. "We play a role and then we forget it," she said later. "It is not a matter of degrading the Negro race. I have seen many of our white friends play roles of different periods and classes." Louise portrayed maids as *characters*. She gave a sense of the person beneath her costume as Mae West's maid in *She Done Him Wrong* (1933), and Jean Harlow's maid in *Bombshell*. "I've worked with most of the stars, yes," said Louise, "but only at the studios, not in domestic service."

Members of the Black community and the Black press criticized actors and actresses like Louise who played demeaning roles. But needing to earn a living, she accepted the parts available to her because she wanted to act in mainstream films instead of "race movies."

In the 1920s, race movies were made outside the Hollywood studios. Black filmmakers such as Oscar Micheaux, wanted to tell realistic stories of African American life to entertain and educate Black movie audiences. The goal was to tackle serious themes and portray "up-lift" dramas. These silent films featured strong, educated men and smart, glamorous women—characters who were the opposite of the stock servants and simpletons depicted in Hollywood films.

But Louise put on her black maid's dress and frilly white headpiece. Again and again she defended her work by saying, "I am only playing the parts. I don't live them."

When silent movies transitioned to talkies in the late 1920s, she got her first role with screen credit in *Coquette* starring Mary Pickford. Louise acted the role of Julia, the family cook, housemaid, and former nanny, who is like a mother to Mary.

For the part of Julia, and roles that came after, Louise had to talk like a Southerner. However, that wasn't the way she spoke. A journalist described Louise's voice as soft, "her accent straight Californian." Louise said, "I had to learn the Negro dialect, just as one learns a foreign language." At first she couldn't even understand that kind of speaking, and kept practicing, and reading books and poems until she had mastered the speech pattern well enough to use it for movies. Today scholars maintain that she was actually taught a "white fabrication of black dialect," which was only accurate in some places.

She needed this accent in *Imitation of Life*, the breakthrough movie in 1934 that established Louise as a star. It was the first time in mainstream American films that a Black woman's problems were given equal importance to those of a white woman. Louise played Delilah Johnson, a housekeeper and cook, and Claudette Colbert, her costar, played the part of widow Bea Pullman, her employer. The two shared screen time throughout the film, a story of single mothers struggling to raise their daughters during the post-Depression era.

Louise Beavers, as the motherly nanny, comforts Mary Pickford in a scene from *Coquette*, 1929. Louise was twenty-seven, ten years younger than Mary.

Louise Beavers on the left as Delilah with Claudette Colbert on the right as Miss Bea in an opening scene from *Imitation of Life*, 1934

In the opening scene, Delilah begs to work for Miss Bea in exchange for room and board for herself and her daughter, Peola. She explains that she doesn't eat too much although she's big. Louise was chosen for the part because of her physical features. She was told to stay overweight during filming in order to look motherly. But the director John Stahl also cast her because she expressed a combination of "warmth and a childlike vulnerability," in contrast to her angry daughter.

Racism is a main theme of the movie. Light-skinned Peola wants to pass for white and resents her mother because of the dark color of her skin even though Delilah gives her a comfortable life. She and "Miss Bea" open a pancake shop that grows into an empire. Their logo features a smiling Delilah in a chef's hat flipping a pancake. Actually, Louise detested cooking and had to learn how to make pancakes. It took five days, and she "became so tired of batter and griddles . . . that she swore that she would never touch another pancake as long as she lived."

The story fast-forwards ten years, and the two women live in a luxurious house, but they both have problems with their daughters. The adult Peola cruelly rejects her mother. Sickened with grief, Delilah dies. At the funeral, Peola realizes what her mother has done for her and begs her forgiveness.

The film was an enormous hit. *Film Daily* wrote, "Put this down as one of the best pictures of the year," and praised Louise's "notable work." *Time* magazine proclaimed that "the real heroine of *Imitation of Life* is not Bea Pullman but Aunt Delilah." California's *Madera Tribune* wrote, "Miss Beavers is excellent in the greatest screen role ever played by a colored person." The Black press

The Boardwalk scene in *Imitation of Life*. From the left:
Louise Beavers with Sebie Hendricks as young Peola, and
Claudette Colbert on the right holding the hand of her
daughter played by Baby Jane as Baby Jessie Pullman,
1934.

cheered Louise for her performance, but also criticized her for portraying a subservient character on the screen.

Off-screen, Louise was anything but subservient. During the filming of *Imitation,* she had insisted a scene be cut because it would have included an offensive derogatory term. The NAACP backed her up and sent a letter to the studio supporting her demand.

The African American press hoped that Louise would win an Oscar for her outstanding performance. But the Academy did not honor her, and the Black press considered it a slight. At that time, there was no category for Best Supporting Actress, which might have given Louise a chance for an award. *California Graphic* magazine stated the real reason for the oversight: "The Academy could not recognize Miss Beavers. She is Black!"

Following the box office success of the movie, Louise found herself in an odd situation. *Imitation of Life* ruined her, said a critic, "because of all idiotic reasons, she was too good!" Louise was the most popular Black actress of her time, and therefore in a class of featured players. So her agent demanded higher salaries for her work, but studios refused to pay. As a result, there were no more great roles for her, and she went back to performing as maids for stars like Carole Lombard, Rosalind Russell, and Myrna Loy. Louise said, "I'd rather play a maid than be one."

Louise worked continuously, and for a while was under contract to a company which produced low-budget movies with all-Black casts, like the old silent race movies. These new films featured well-known stars like Louise, who appealed to mixed audiences. The stories presented realistic situations that dealt with Black issues. In 1939's *Reform School,* Louise starred as Mother Barton,

Louise Beavers as Mother Barton at her desk helps
wayward boys in *Reform School*, 1939.

the warden of an all-boys reformatory. She was billed in ads as
"First Lady of the Screen," and toured nationally wearing a stylish
hat and fur coat. A critic for the *Washington Afro-American* hailed
Louise's performance, writing that she "comes through with flying
colors in a story especially written for her. She turns in a dramatic
triumph."

Louise earned enough money to buy a house in Los Angeles
and hire a maid. Contrary to her roles on-screen, Louise hated
housework. Later, in the early 1940s, she moved to a grander three-

story house, which had once belonged to a mayor of Los Angeles, in a section called Sugar Hill. The area was named for the legendary Sugar Hill neighborhood in Harlem, New York, which was home to Black celebrities. Sugar Hill in Los Angeles became a gathering place for Black Hollywood stars and visiting entertainers. Louise and her guests enjoyed playing poker on the third floor. Her husband, Leroy Moore, a chef and interior decorator from Texas, prepared and helped serve the refreshments. And she rented rooms to her fellow performers for extra income.

Louise and Black movie stars had settled in Sugar Hill despite a deed drawn up by racist white residents in 1938 prohibiting ownership by non-whites. By 1945, at the end of World War II, eight white homeowners sued to have Louise and fifty-seven other Black families evicted. Louise refused to accept racism off-screen and was one of the leaders of a group of Black homeowners who fought back. They met at her house every Saturday for workshops to map out their strategy with the help of a civil rights lawyer from the NAACP. The "Sugar Hill" case came to trial on December 5, 1945, with Louise as one of the ten codefendants.

The attorneys for the white plaintiffs demanded that Louise and her Black neighbors give up their homes right away. Louise's lawyer argued that the racist restrictive deeds violated rights guaranteed under the Fourteenth Amendment to the Constitution. The judge agreed and threw the case out of court. He said, "It is time that members of the Negro race are accorded, without reservations and evasions, the full rights guaranteed them under the 14th amendment of the Federal Constitution." His ruling set an important precedent in the ongoing battle to end residential segregation in the United States.

During her long career as an actress as well as an activist, Louise appeared in more than 260 movies. She even worked in television in the early 1950s as Beulah, the title character of a weekly comedy series, playing another maid who helps solve her white employers' problems.

But it was her achievement in *Imitation of Life* that paved the way for Black actresses to reach higher levels of screen roles in Hollywood. Louise participated in creating "Black stardom," wrote a film scholar. After her death in 1962, Louise was inducted into the newly formed Black Filmmakers Hall of Fame. An audience of three thousand attended the event. Among the fifteen inductees that evening were Diahann Carroll, Ethel Waters, and Harry Belafonte. When the emcee opened the program, he said, the purpose of the organization was "to honor those who have been overlooked by the white awards ceremonies, and those who have made a significant contribution to Black people."

That introduction perfectly described Louise Beavers.

Louise Beavers as Delilah tries to win the love of her daughter, the adult Peola, played by Fredi Washington, in *Imitation of Life*, 1934.

CHAPTER 5 FREDI WASHINGTON

"I AM A NEGRO AND I AM PROUD OF IT."   —Fredi Washington

A ctress Fredericka Carolyn "Fredi" Washington's real life changed when she was cast in the blockbuster movie *Imitation of Life*. She played her biggest role as the adult Peola—the daughter of the dark-skinned Delilah—who passes as white. Fredi identified as Black. "No matter how white I look," she said, "on the inside I feel black. . . . I am proud to be a Negro."

Although Fredi played the daughter of Louise Beavers in the movie, she was only one year younger. Fredi was born on December 23, 1903, in Savannah, Georgia. Her mother—a former dancer—was a homemaker, and her father was a postal worker. Both of her parents were of African American and European ancestry. Fredi was the oldest of their five children. Her mother died in 1914, when Fredi was eleven, and when Fredi's father remarried in 1917, she and her sister Isabel were sent to a convent school for Black girls in Pennsylvania, which stressed social justice and resistance to racism.

From there they went to Harlem, New York, to live with their grandmother known as "Big Mama." Fredi graduated from Julia Richman High School and continued studying at Egri School of Dramatic Writing and the Christophe School of Languages. To earn a living, she worked as a secretary at W. C. Handy's Black Swan Records. Handy was an African American composer of hits such as "St. Louis Blues," and his company recorded jazz and blues. There

73

she heard about auditions for the all-Black Broadway revue *Shuffle Along*. Although Fredi didn't consider herself a dancer, and had no professional training, she tried out and was hired. After touring with the show for two years, she landed a role as a leading lady in the Broadway play *Black Boy*, starring Paul Robeson, a famous and influential Black singer and actor.

Fredi kept working in theater and in films, and was cast as the leading lady in the short musical movie *Black and Tan*, with bandleader Duke Ellington. During filming, Fredi had met Lawrence Brown, a trombonist with the band, and the two would become a couple.

Fredi Washington and Duke Ellington in the musical short
Black and Tan, 1929

In 1933, Fredi appeared with Paul Robeson again in a movie version of Eugene O'Neill's play *The Emperor Jones*. It was a mainstream talkie in the early days of motion pictures with sound. Fredi and Robeson felt comfortable speaking on camera because of their work in the theater. The story told of a Black Pullman porter, Brutus Jones, who kills a man, goes to prison, and escapes to a Caribbean Island where he proclaims himself emperor. Fredi played the part of Jones's sultry girlfriend. However, when the censors viewed the daily rushes, she looked so light they worried that audiences might think Robeson was romantic with a white actress, a taboo in the Jim Crow era, a period known for segregation, for restricting the rights of African Americans. Most states prohibited miscegenation—interracial love and marriage. Because Fredi's skin had to be darkened with makeup for the film, she had mixed feelings about the role, but it launched her career as a movie actress.

Soon after Lawrence Brown and she were married (in August 1933), Fredi got a call from Universal asking her to come to New York and test for the role of Peola in *Imitation of Life*. She didn't know that the director, John Stahl, was searching for the right Black actress who could pass for white. He could have chosen a white actress for the part, as many directors would have done, but he was determined to find "a young girl who must be of Negro blood" who looked Caucasian. His search aroused great interest in Black Hollywood. An item in *The California Eagle* read, "Noted Director on Strangest Casting Mission on Record." Stahl considered three hundred women for the part, but he kept remembering Fredi's performance in a couple of films and was struck by her looks as well as her

Fredi Washington snuggles up to Brutus Jones, played by Paul Robeson in *The Emperor Jones*, 1933.

"distinct presence." Most of all, she "projected intelligence," and he believed that she would bring that quality to the role.

After Fredi's screen test, she heard nothing. Four months later, when she and her husband arrived in Los Angeles for him to perform with Duke Ellington's band, she was called back to Universal for another test. Stahl gave her the script of *Imitation of Life* and asked for her comments.

Fredi found that some of the screenplay gave a false picture of African Americans. She objected to a ridiculous scene in the script when the adult Peola works as a cashier in a restaurant and is discovered to be Black from the lack of half moons for cuticles on her fingernails. Fredi met with Stahl and said, "There are a few things you better get straightened out." She showed him her cuticles with moons, and he understood. The script was changed, and Stahl immediately gave her the part. Because she was Black, her casting was considered groundbreaking.

When Fredi reviewed her contract, she had more objections. Universal executives wanted to sign her up for five or seven years, the dream of most young actresses. Not Fredi. "I don't know if I would be good in the movies," she told them since she had played only minor roles. "And if I'm not good, I don't want to be in the movies." The studio executives said if she were under contract she could train for a career in films. But Fredi said, "I didn't come out here to learn to act. I brought that with me. I've been on Broadway." She knew that if the movie was a success, they probably wouldn't have another good script for her, and she'd wind up playing "some dim-witted maid" because of her contractual agreement. "Let's talk about *Imitation of Life*," she said. "This is what I'm interested in now."

Claudette Colbert on the right tries to persuade the tearful Peola, played by Fredi Washington, to accept her mother in *Imitation of Life*, 1934.

Next they discussed her salary. She named the figure she wanted. But the executives said they weren't paying Louise Beavers that much, and she was the star. Fredi said that Louise's business had nothing to do with her. Finally they gave Fredi the $500 a week that she demanded. But they were astonished when she insisted that her lawyer review the contract before she signed. "They just hadn't dealt before with anyone like me in our race," she said. Finally, Universal let Fredi send the contract to her lawyer to look it over. "And if he thinks it looks all right," she said, "then I'll be kind enough to put my signature on this piece of paper." He approved and she signed.

Fredi and Louise were so different that Hollywood gossips expected them to clash. Fredi was a New York stage actress, whereas Louise was a Hollywood actress, with a hundred movies to her credit. But surprisingly, the two women became close friends. When Fredi's husband left to travel with Ellington, she stayed at Louise's home during filming. Louise introduced Fredi to the Black Hollywood crowd, and pointed out who the gossips were, and who to impress. Often they'd drive to the studio together and go through the routine of makeup, hair, and wardrobe before shooting a scene.

On the set, Fredi questioned a line of dialogue in one of the scenes. Peola is supposed to look in the mirror and say she wants to be white. For Fredi, this interpretation was wrong, and she told Stahl that she couldn't read those words. She said, "I always felt that Peola didn't want to be white. She wanted *white opportunities*," just like the daughter of her mother's employer. The two girls had grown up in the same household. Stahl agreed with Fredi and let her play the scene her way.

Released in December 1934, the film received an Academy nomination for Outstanding Production (later called Best Picture). Although it didn't win, *Imitation of Life* raised heated discussion about race in America. The *Literary Digest* applauded Fredi's portrayal of a biracial woman as "vital, straightforward, and splendidly in earnest." The *New York Amsterdam News* said, "Fredi Washington expresses the desire for freedom and equal justice in this picture that is more convincing than any mere performer could have voiced." Critics pointed out that Fredi had been denied a fuller choice of film roles up till then because of racial prejudice.

Some reviewers and moviegoers claimed that Fredi's

performance was so believable because she was really like the character, Peola. Fredi kept denying these opinions. "I have never tried to pass for white and never had any desire to do so," she told the *Chicago Defender*. "In 'Imitation of Life,' I was showing how a girl might feel under the circumstances, but I am not showing how I feel myself." She added, "I am proud of my race."

Fredi insisted that as an actress, she was merely playing a part on the screen. "Peola, who desires whiteness, is a character created by white people."

The role of Peola haunted Fredi. Again and again she needed to distance herself from the movie and publicly assert her views. "Why should I have to pass for anything but an artist?" she said. "When I act, I live the role I am assigned to do." Fredi launched a campaign to protest rumors that she and Peola were the same.

Despite the interest in Fredi, and accolades for her work, no studio offered her a great follow-up role. She appeared as a biracial woman raising a white child as her own in *One Mile from Heaven*, a 1937 film. Critics praised Fredi as "splendid. Has looks. Good voice and real acting ability. She's deserving of a better chance than this picture offers."

Fredi thought so too and returned to New York, where she became politically active. Her experiences in the film industry and theater inspired her to speak out about racism faced by African Americans. In 1937, she cofounded the Negro Actors Guild of America (NAG) with Paul Robeson, composers Noble Sissle (of *Shuffle Along*) and W. C. Handy, and actress Ethel Waters. Their goal was to help Black actors find more opportunities, and wider ranges of roles, and to protest stereotyping.

She worked closely with Walter White, then president of the NAACP, in his crusade to pass anti-lynching legislation. Since the Civil War, thousands of African American men and women were killed in violent lynchings. After news of a lynching, a flag flew from the window of the NAACP headquarters in New York with the words "A Man Was Lynched Yesterday." Fredi showed her support by wearing a black armband in an anti-lynching demonstration in February 1938. The *New York Herald Tribune* described her at age thirty-five as "a frail, defenseless ingénue by night—a forthright, uncompromising crusader by day."

Fredi used the press to express her views. She was intolerant of discrimination in all levels of American society. She condemned the vicious system of Jim Crow laws. Most of all, she criticized the entertainment industry for perpetuating racial stereotypes and projecting false attitudes about African Americans. Fredi maintained that entertainers shared the responsibility of elevating the Black image on the stage and screen.

"Who said art is not in politics?" she asked. "It is indeed, and it is here to stay."

Fredi's legacy lives on in Oscar- and Emmy-winning actress Regina King. Like Fredi, King is "using her spotlight to speak out on social justice." "As a Black woman she reflects on all of the struggles Black Americans have been through." In an interview with *Glamour* magazine, King said that the 2020 Black Lives Matter Protest gave her "hope."

"It feels like people are paying attention."

Hattie McDaniel in Denver, Colorado, after winning a national radio contest for reciting "Convict Joe," about 1911

HATTIE McDANIEL

"I'm a fine Black mammy [on the screen]. But I'm Hattie McDaniel in my house."
—Hattie McDaniel

attie McDaniel sang before she acted. As a little girl, she sang so much that her mother said, "Hattie, I'll pay you to hush," and gave her a dime. "But in just a few minutes," remembered Hattie, "I'd be singing and shouting again." At age six she decided to become an actress. "I always wanted to be before the public," she said.

Hattie was born on June 10, 1893, in Wichita, Kansas, the youngest of thirteen children. Only half her siblings survived, either dying at birth or soon after. Both of her parents had been born into slavery. Her father, Henry McDaniel, fled a plantation and joined the Union army when the Civil War broke out. Later, in 1878, he married Susan Holbert Staton, a widow in Nashville, Tennessee. She was a gospel singer and a deeply religious woman. Fighting poverty, the family kept moving to places where Henry could find jobs. From Wichita they traveled to Fort Collins, Colorado, and then settled in Denver, which had a strong Black community, when Hattie was five. Yet most Black families like Hattie's lived in poor neighborhoods.

Susan worked in white homes and took Hattie along to help. At an early age Hattie learned how to cook, clean, and do laundry. Although Denver's schools were not segregated, Hattie was one of the few Black children in her class. Her favorite teacher let her stand in front of the room and sing and recite poetry. Years later, when Hattie became a well-known performer, her teacher wrote to her and said, "I recall with pleasure the keen enjoyment of the pupils and myself whenever you sang or dramatized a story."

At East Denver High School, Hattie was always chosen for plays and musical productions. She loved performing popular dances such as the cakewalk, juba, and soft-shoe buck. When she was fifteen, in 1908, she entered a drama contest sponsored by the Women's Temperance League. Hattie emotionally recited a poem titled "Convict Joe," about the evils of alcoholism, and wowed the judges. She won the gold medal, and the sound of applause thrilled her. Now she knew that she was destined to be a performer.

Her older brothers Otis and Sam were also musically talented. When Otis formed his own theatrical troupe, he persuaded their mother to let Hattie go on tour with them. Their father, a banjo and guitar player, supported the idea. "There is so much trouble in this world, I hope you will pray that through you the Lord will make people happy," he told her. And she did, dropping out of school in her sophomore year and happily touring from Colorado to Oklahoma. Back in Denver, Hattie worked as a servant and took in laundry as "a means to an end." Later she said this was an "honorable way to make an honest dollar," as she struggled to build her career.

When she was seventeen, she met and fell in love with Howard Hickman, a gifted pianist. He was the first African American pianist in Denver hired to accompany silent films in movie houses. They married on January 19, 1911. During the week they did their regular jobs. He was a laborer for a mining supply company. But on days and nights off, they pursued their artistic talents. Hattie organized an all-female minstrel show with her sister Etta. Playing for Black audiences, she spoofed the blackface minstrel tradition of white entertainers darkening their faces to portray racial stereotypes. She too darkened her face with burnt cork, and created an exaggerated mammy character—silly, sassy, and bold. Hattie was developing comedy traits that she would use in her movie roles.

When Hattie's husband became ill four years later and died of pneumonia, Hattie became overwhelmed with grief and stopped performing. The following year, her brother Otis died. In memory of him, Hattie and Etta revived their all-women minstrel troupe and put on their routines. But opportunities in segregated Denver were limited for Black performers. California's growing film industry seemed a little more promising. Etta and their brother Sam, taking a chance on getting work as extras, moved to Los Angeles.

Hattie remained in Denver and became a blues singer with George Morrison's band, the Melody Hounds. She and Morrison put together an act combining music and comedy, and toured theaters on the vaudeville circuit throughout the United States, which featured all kinds of entertainers—singers, dancers, jugglers, magicians, and more.

Back home, they won a date on Denver's KOA Monday *Radio Concerts,* and Hattie boasted that she was the first African American woman to perform on the radio with an orchestra. Despite her success, Denver didn't have much more to offer her, so Hattie left for Chicago. Over the next few years she worked as a cook, maid, and waitress between gigs as a singer and comedienne. She wrote songs such as "Boo Hoo Blues" that were recorded on OKeh's Race Records, the first major label for African Americans.

Hattie's singing captured attention, and she won a part in the Jubilee Chorus of the hit musical *Show Boat*. After a fifteen-week run in Chicago, the show left for a road tour, but unfortunately the country had plunged into the Great Depression. By the time the touring company reached Milwaukee, the producer couldn't afford to keep a large cast and laid off Hattie. "I landed there broke," she recalled.

Hattie didn't give up. She soon found work as a restroom attendant at an inn for seven dollars a week plus tips. The inn featured a nightly floorshow, and the ladies' room was near the stage. One night the band needed a vocalist. Hattie stepped in and sang "St. Louis Blues." The customers gave her a standing ovation, plus ninety dollars in tips. That night the manager hired Hattie to sing. "I never had to go back to my maid's job," she recalled.

But in 1931, thirty-eight-year-old Hattie packed her things, and with twenty dollars in her purse, drove west with a few friends to join her brother and sister in Hollywood and try the movies.

Sam had his own band and had become a radio personality. Through his connections, Hattie sang a solo with Sara Butler's Old Time Southern Singers, a popular choral group, and was a sensation. Butler's husband, Charles, ran the Central Casting Agency that placed Black performers in mainstream movies, and Hattie paid him a visit. Butler looked for "types." Hattie's dark skin and large figure matched the image of a maid that producers demanded, and she immediately began working as an extra for $7.50 a day. Sometimes the movie called for a mammy, a stereotypical servant. Still, Hattie was elated to fit the bill. "A call from Charles Butler at Central Casting was like a letter from

From left: Etta, Sam, and Hattie McDaniel disembark from a railroad car in Los Angeles, about 1931 or 1940.

home," she said. For the next three years she appeared as an extra in hundreds of films, while performing with the Old Time Southern Singers and working as a laundress.

Hattie's real break came in 1932 when she had a speaking part in *Blonde Venus* (1932), a talkie starring Marlene Dietrich. Hattie played a maid, but not the usual meek sort. She drew from her experiences in minstrel parodies and as a blues singer and acted fearless on-screen.

Actress Hattie McDaniel at her dressing table mirror, 1940

The performance led to her first studio contract two years later to act with Will Rogers, the popular film star, in *Judge Priest*, and sing in the movie. Rogers was so pleased with her performance as a housekeeper that he requested that she improvise a song with him. From then on, Hattie worked steadily bringing a comic, brassy style to the stereotypical roles she portrayed.

Good parts for African American actresses were scarce. Louise Beavers was the biggest name at that time, and though she and Hattie competed for the same roles, they became close friends. During the *Imitation of Life* auditions, Hattie desperately wanted to be cast as Delilah. It was the first dramatic starring role offered to a Black actress. Although Louise got the part, Hattie won her biggest role yet—as Mom Beck, an obedient mammy, in the 1935 film *The Little Colonel* starring Shirley Temple, the most famous child star of the day. Even at age six, little Shirley realized the depth of racial prejudice in this movie, and later wrote about it in her memoir.

Due to the small number of roles available to them, Hattie and Louise kept vying for the same parts. Hollywood insiders predicted that Hattie would become more renowned when Universal cast her as Queenie in the 1936 movie *Show Boat*. Hattie was thrilled and honored to perform with Paul Robeson who reprised his stage role as Queenie's husband, Joe. She provided flashes of humor that contrasted with his powerful delivery of songs such as "Ol' Man River." Robeson complimented her and told the *California Eagle* that Hattie "was one of the best actresses he ever met."

With the success of *Show Boat*, Hattie bought her first house, complete with a grand piano and collection of books on Black history and culture. Unlike Louise, she enjoyed cooking and

Hattie McDaniel as Queenie and Paul Robeson as her
husband Joe in the movie *Show Boat*, 1936

loved entertaining at home. Off-screen she was known as "a very
fashionable dresser." Like Louise, Hattie stressed the difference
between her real self and the roles she played. "I'm a fine Black
mammy [on the screen]," she told aspiring actress Lena Horne. "But
I'm Hattie McDaniel in my house."

Although Hattie resented these typecast roles, her career was
booming. In 1938, Hollywood buzzed with excitement over the
forthcoming movie *Gone with the Wind*, based on the best seller
by Margaret Mitchell. Caught up in the frenzy, Hattie immediately
bought the novel, a historical epic romance set in the Old South

during the Civil War and Reconstruction era. The story told of Scarlett O'Hara, the spoiled, vain daughter of the owner of Tara, a cotton plantation in Georgia. Scarlett is in love with Ashley Wilkes, but he is engaged to his cousin Melanie. Heartbroken, Scarlett eventually marries Rhett Butler, a charming gambler and blockade runner for the Confederacy.

Producer David O. Selznick immediately chose Clark Gable as Rhett Butler, but he interviewed 1,400 women nationwide for Scarlett. Competition was also intense for the role of Scarlett's loyal mammy. Even First Lady Eleanor Roosevelt recommended her personal maid. Hattie was determined to get the part. She knew her friend Louise was her biggest rival. Selznick received letters supporting Louise for the role, and she seemed likely to get it. Clark Gable favored his friend Hattie McDaniel. They had appeared together in a 1935 comedy *China Seas,* and he thought she'd be great.

Hattie arrived dressed as a typical old Southern mammy for her screen test on December 6, 1938. She had carefully read the book and acquired a Georgia accent. In her screen test, she tightened Scarlett's corset and scolded her for eating too much. And she warned Scarlett about making a fool of herself over the handsome but unavailable Ashley. Hattie's bossy manner and booming voice were perfect. When she finished her audition, Selznick cancelled all the other actresses, and on January 27, 1939, he offered Hattie a contract for $450 a week. She was forty-five.

During filming, tensions arose. Many Black leaders worried about the demeaning portrayal of their people—with the enslaved characters presented as preferring their bondage to freedom. Walter White of the NAACP suggested that an African American

Vivien Leigh as Scarlett O'Hara and Hattie McDaniel as Mammy in *Gone with the Wind*, 1939

consultant oversee the production. Selznick sympathized with White but decided against it. He assured White that Hattie's character Mammy, for example, "is treated very lovably and with great dignity."

Yet, protests against the movie continued throughout production. By fall 1939, shooting had finally been completed. Selznick personally congratulated Hattie for her "brilliant performance." Author Margaret Mitchell sent her a set of Wedgewood teacups and saucers painted with Atlanta landmarks. However, when the movie premiered in Atlanta, Hattie couldn't attend because of Jim Crow segregation in the South. Even her image was removed from the program. Hattie accepted the situation gracefully and never commented to protect her career.

But in February 1940, she earned recognition for her sensational performance. The Academy of Motion Picture Arts and Sciences nominated Hattie as Best Supporting Actress. The ceremony happened at the Cocoanut Grove ballroom of Hollywood's Ambassador Hotel. On the night of the presentations, Hattie was decked out in a blue evening gown, an ermine wrap, and gardenias in her hair. Unable to sit with her white costars because the hotel was segregated, she and her agent and escort were seated at the back of the ballroom. When Hattie was announced the winner of the Oscar for Best Supporting Actress, the crowd of 17,000 went wild. The entire audience "stood and cheered their beloved Hattie McDaniel," remembered an observer. Tears came to Hattie's eyes as she made her way to the stage to accept her award, which she called, "one of the happiest moments of my life."

Hattie was the first African American to receive an Academy Award. "Black Hollywood was ecstatic," wrote a film historian. Days later Hattie told a newspaper that she hoped her award [a plaque for winners in that category until 1943] would encourage young Black people "to aim high and work hard." She said, "I consider this recognition a step further for the race, rather than personal progress."

The next Black actress to win an Academy award came sixty-two years later. In her acceptance speech for her role in the 2001 film *Monster's Ball*, Halle Berry said, "This moment is so much bigger than me. . . . It's for every nameless, faceless woman of color that now has a chance because this door tonight has been opened." Although Berry didn't mention Hattie, another Black actress would.

In 2010, Monique Angela Hicks, known professionally as Mo'Nique, won an Oscar for Best Supporting Actress for her

Hattie McDaniel, winner of the Academy Award for Best Supporting Actress in *Gone with the Wind,* with her plaque, 1940

performance in *Precious* (2009). That evening she wore a blue dress and gardenias in her hair just as Hattie had done back in 1940. Upon receiving her award Mo'Nique said, "I want to thank Miss Hattie McDaniel for enduring all that she had to so that I would not have to." Backstage, Mo'Nique said, "Miss Hattie McDaniel, I feel you all over me, and it's about time the whole world felt you all over them."

Hattie McDaniel at the microphone in Hollywood playing the lead in her hit radio series *Beulah*, 1947

Portrait of Marion Wong that appeared in newspapers and
Moving Picture World, 1917

CHAPTER 7 MARION WONG

"I DECIDED THAT PEOPLE WHO ARE INTERESTED IN MY PEOPLE AND MY COUNTRY WOULD LIKE TO SEE SOME OF THE CUSTOMS AND MANNERS OF CHINA."
—Marion Wong

Over a hundred years ago, Marion Evelyn Wong, a young woman in Oakland, California, dared to make a movie. She opened her own movie company and created a silent film: *The Curse of Quon Gwon: When the Far East Mingles with the West*. It was the earliest known Chinese American movie. Marion's film portrayed the problems of real Chinese Americans like her family and friends in the early twentieth century who tried to blend in with other Americans while honoring their ancient culture and traditions.

One of the many challenges Marion faced in making a movie was prejudice. Whites often taunted Chinese Americans and called them ugly names due to resentment and fear. A popular anti-Chinese slogan of the era was "They Must Go."

Marion stood fast. She was determined to make her film.

As a third-generation Chinese American, she wanted to present a true and sympathetic picture of her people. In an interview with the *Oakland Tribune* in 1916, she said, "I had never seen any Chinese movies, so I decided to introduce them to the world." Marion had indeed seen many movies since her father's restaurant was near the local movie theaters. She was a girl with "imagination, executive ability, wit and beauty."

Marion was born in San Francisco's Chinatown on January 2, 1895, the youngest of six. Of all the children she was the closest to her mother, Chin See, who had also been born in San Francisco. Marion's family was wealthy and had close ties to business and city leaders.

Her father, Jim Sing Wong, had migrated to California from the Guangdong Province in China in 1869 during the years of the Gold Rush. He married Chin See when she was fifteen. When the earthquake and fire of 1906 struck San Francisco, Chinatown was destroyed. Marion's family lost their money and connections just as many other Chinese immigrants did. They ended up moving to Oakland and opened a restaurant, Edvin's Oriental Café, in the busy downtown theater district. From an early age Marion waited tables and worked as a cashier. Neighborhood theaters gave her a chance to see silent movies and vaudeville shows.

At sixteen her budding fondness for show business was cut short when she sailed to Hong Kong with her parents and brother Albert. Her parents intended for Marion to marry a banker and for Albert to find a wife—a common practice among Chinese American families at that time. Although the Wongs were American citizens, they had to carry identification cards according to the Geary Act, which required all persons of Chinese descent, including those who were born in the United States, like Marion and her mother, to carry photo IDs.

Instead of embarking from the San Francisco pier like other Americans, the Wongs were treated as if they were criminals and questioned for hours on Angel Island, an immigration center. Required to present statements from friends, relatives, and white witnesses, the Wongs had to prove that they were good citizens before they could board their ship.

While the Wongs were in Hong Kong in 1911, the Chinese Revolution broke out in the southern part of China's mainland. Sun Yat-sen and rebels overthrew the Empress and the imperial dynasty and established the Republic of China. Being there at such an exciting time stirred Marion's Chinese pride and imagination. Later she used the revolution as part of her film. During these historic events, Albert met Violet Jang Mon Foo, their marriage was arranged, and they wed in Hong Kong. However, Marion bucked tradition. She refused to marry the man chosen for her, and her mother supported her decision.

Marion and her sister-in-law Violet, who was also sixteen, became lifelong best friends back home. They would go to Western hotels wearing traditional *cheongsam* dresses and dance with each other, pretending to be princesses from China. Wong also began performing as a singer at Oakland theaters and had billing at one theater as "Princess Marian [*sic*] Wong, the Chinese Song Bird."

Marion continued to work in her parents' restaurant. A steady customer was Charlie Chaplin, who was directing and acting in films shot in Oakland. He and the cast and crew ate meals at Edvin's Café, which stayed open from morning till late at night. According to family lore, Marion became interested in their film work and asked Chaplin's cameraman for advice about equipment.

Despite her lack of training or experience, Marion ambitiously began her film project in 1916 when she was twenty-one. "I first wrote the love story," she told the *Oakland Tribune*. Most likely it was inspired by Violet's marriage to her brother and departure from

Marion Wong on the left, and her sister-in-law Violet on the right perform as Chinese princesses, about 1916.

her homeland. "Then," said Marion, "I decided that people who are interested in my people and my country would like to see some of the customs and manners of China. So I added to the love drama many scenes depicting these things. I do hope it will be a success." Although the movie was set in California, a subplot involved the Chinese Revolution. Some characters in her film were spies secretly loyal to the Chinese monarchy, and others were "working for the revolutionists in favor of a Chinese republic," noted *Moving Picture World*.

Marion wrote the script and directed the movie. She explained the plot in a movie magazine: "*The Curse of Quon Gwon* deals with the curse of a Chinese god that follows his people because of the influence of Western civilization." The main story tells of a young Chinese American couple who are cursed for not following tradition but become modern Americans in the end.

Marion needed funding for her production, so she went to her older sister Alice's husband, a prosperous Chinatown merchant. He raised money from all of her family, including Marion's brother Albert. Everyone donated what they could so that she and her parents could form the Mandarin Film Company, the first Chinese American film company.

Marion built a makeshift studio behind her family's house, borrowed Chinese furniture and props from local shops and homes, rented camera equipment, and hired production assistants. Her sisters Alice and Rose were coproducers in charge of costumes, makeup, and hairstyling. The cast of thirty was entirely Chinese and starred members of her family. Her sister-in-law Violet played the heroine, her mother Chin See played the interfering mother-in-law,

Scene from *The Curse of Quon Gwon*. From left, Violet
Wong, an unidentified cast member, Wong's mother Chin
See, and actor Harvey Soo Hoo, 1917.

a family friend took the role of bridegroom, and even Violet's three-year-old daughter Stella had a part. Marion cast herself as the mean troublemaker.

Marion proudly presented a rough cut (the first edited version) of the movie to family and friends before it premiered at Oakland's Kinema Theater in May 1917. A local newspaper reported, "Los Angeles may be the center of the motion picture world, but Oakland has the honor of producing the first Chinese film drama."

That summer Marion and her mother traveled to New York City to market the film to national distributors. As an independent producer, Marion needed a company to show the film to movie theater owners who would order prints and advertise the film. But none of them was willing to screen the movie. They didn't believe that mainstream audiences would like a Chinese American story that did not include the usual stereotypes—gamblers, opium addicts, and mysterious "Oriental" women.

The Curse was in fact cursed. Without distribution and the possibility of earning money to repay investors, the Mandarin Film Company closed. Marion's brother-in-law declared bankruptcy and was disgraced. All the relatives who had contributed to the production "lost face"—they had lost their pride in the eyes of others. They felt embarrassed and dishonored. Marion was so discouraged by her failure that she asked the family to never speak of the film again.

Marion put moviemaking behind her and married Kin Seung Hong, the first Chinese student to graduate from the University of California, Berkeley, and one of the first Chinese electrical engineers in the country. And she and her husband raised six children.

Violet combs her hair before the wedding in *The Curse of Quon Gwon,* **1917.**

For years, *The Curse* remained hidden away and forgotten. One Saturday in 1968, Violet's grandson, Gregory Yee Mark, a college student majoring in Asian American studies, visited her in Berkeley. Violet took him down to the basement of her house and pointed toward a large canister in a corner. "Gregory," she said, "there's an old film in this box—you go do something with it."

Mark later had the reels transferred to 16mm film, but only half the film could be saved. Mark was ecstatic as he watched what was left of the feature movie. "Three generations of women in my family were involved in the film," he exclaimed. Marion had died in 1969, and after Violet's death, the film went to Mark, and other members of the family. Eventually it made its way to the University of California, Berkeley, Asian American Studies Library.

In 2006 the Library of Congress selected Marion's film to be added to the National Film Registry, which honors movies that are important to the history of American films and cultural history. *The Curse* is the only film that authentically shows the lives of Chinese Americans in 1916, while meeting the highest standards of professional filmmaking.

Marion had thought she was a failure, but she wasn't. Shown at film festivals and conferences in Oakland, Hollywood, and venues around the world, *The Curse* is hailed as a masterpiece. There, in black and white, Marion's cast and crew bring her original story to life. *The Curse* lives on.

Portrait of Anna May Wong by Carl Van Vechten,
September 22, 1935

CHAPTER 8 ANNA MAY WONG

"I WOULD BECOME A MOVIE STAR TOO."   —Anna May Wong

Anna May Wong was the first major Chinese American movie star who rose to international fame. But Anna had humble beginnings, working alongside her mother, sisters, and brothers in her father's laundry.

Anna, the second oldest of five children, was born in Los Angeles, California, on January 3, 1905, as Wong Liu Tsong, which means Yellow Frosted Willow in Cantonese. At school she was given the European name Anna. When she grew older, she added May. "It made a prettier signature," she said, "and I liked the suggestion of springtime in May."

Anna grew up in her father's laundry a few blocks away from Chinatown. Her father, Sam Sing Wong, had been born in Michigan Bluffs near Sacramento, where *his* father had opened a store during the Gold Rush. Sam had worked in the gold mines, then sailed to China to find a wife. He married and had a son, and returned to California, hoping to earn enough money to bring his wife and baby to America. But U.S. Immigration policies prevented his wife from entering the country. Wong later wrote in her memoir that it was customary for Chinese men in that era to marry more than once. While her father's first wife remained in China, he remarried in California.

His second wife, Gon Toy Lee, was a sixteen-year-old Chinese American from San Francisco, and they raised a family in two rooms behind the laundry. As soon as they were old enough, Anna, Lulu, and their brother James hauled baskets of dirty laundry to their father's shop and helped their parents with washing and ironing.

Anna and her brothers and sisters played happily with neighborhood children who came from English, Canadian, German, Spanish, Mexican, Russian, and Polish families who had settled in America. But at public school, Lulu and Anna experienced racism. One day when they were going home, a bunch of boys chased them, shouting, "Chink, Chink, Chinaman." The girls ran to the laundry crying. Their father said that although the remarks were meant to shame them, they should always be proud of their people and race.

But Anna never forgot the hurt. Though she and Lulu were bullied, their white teachers and administrators were prejudiced against them and did nothing to help them. "We lived in such terror," recalled Anna. "We became ill with fright."

To protect Anna and Lulu, their parents enrolled them in the Chinese Mission School in Chinatown, which had only Chinese American students. Their father also wanted them to study the Cantonese language and history and culture of China, so he sent them to a Chinese language school after their regular classes ended.

Walking from one school to the other, Wong and her sister often passed movie crews. "We were always thrilled when a motion picture company came down into Chinatown to film scenes for a picture," said Anna. She would push her way through the crowd to get close to the cameras and stare at the glamorous actresses. During shooting breaks, she pestered the director and cameraman with questions, and they nicknamed her "C.C.C." for "Curious Chinese Child."

By age eleven, Anna had decided on her career. "Yes, I would become a movie star too." She saved her lunch money and played hooky from school to see movies at the nickelodeons. When she was fourteen, she had her first break. Actor James Wang, her father's friend, was also a casting agent who helped the studio hire Chinese Americans for bit parts. When Metro Studio needed lantern carriers for the silent movie *The Red Lantern*, Wang took Anna.

"The studio was an enchanted fairyland to me," recalled Anna, "and though I was only an extra, I felt sure that I'd see my name in electric lights before too long."

To prepare for her first movie role, Anna made herself up with her mother's rice powder rag, rouged her cheeks with wet red paper, and curled her hair. When she arrived on the set the director was horrified and told two costume women to wash her hair and scrub off her makeup because she was supposed to look like a peasant.

When the movie came out in 1919, Wong skipped lunch and saved her pennies so that she could take a few girls with her "to witness my triumph." They sat in the balcony and when the movie showed three Chinese girls walking with lanterns in the dim light, Wong's friends asked, "Which one is you?"

"I don't know," she replied. "I could not find myself at all."

But Anna didn't get discouraged. She cut classes to go to the movies, and forged excuse notes from her teacher. When her father found out, he spanked her with a bamboo stick. "You have to go to school and not always play hooky," he shouted.

But that didn't stop her.

Anna told Wang how she dreamed of becoming a movie actress and begged him to find more bit parts for her. "Your eyes are large and your features stand out clearly," he said. "There is no reason why you should not make good if you are willing to work hard." "I am sure you will not go unnoticed."

Directors did notice her. At fifteen, Anna was beautiful, with long shining black hair. She secretly visited the back lots of Hollywood studios and was cast as an extra in the 1920 silent movie *Dinty*, and many other films. Only her sisters and brothers knew about her movie work.

Although he was friends with Wang, her father disapproved of acting as a suitable profession for his daughter since there were no Asian American female role models in Hollywood. However, director Marshall Neilan became so captivated by Wong's performance in *Dinty*, that he wrote the role of Toy Sing for her in *Bits of Life* (1921). Everything changed.

"Of course my parents had to know, presently that I was doing screen work," said Anna, "and I had it out then and there with my father. He said I was disgracing his family, but I told him that I was determined to be independent some day, that I just couldn't be like the girls who live in China." He wanted her to have a steady job as a secretary and then marry a Chinese American man.

Her mother objected, too. "Anna May," she said, "I wish you would not have so many photographs taken. Eventually you may lose your soul."

Her father finally accepted her goal to be in movies if he could escort her to the studio and if she finished her education. Anna enrolled in Los Angeles High School and majored in art, but she

Lon Chaney strangles Anna May Wong in a scene from *Bits of Life*, 1921. Off-screen they were friends.

left at age sixteen before graduating to pursue her Hollywood career.

At five feet seven, Wong was unusually tall and graceful. In between acting jobs, she modeled furs. As an elegant Chinese American posing in expensive clothes for newspaper advertisements, Anna broke racial barriers. And she got noticed.

At seventeen, she won the lead in *The Toll of the Sea*, a 1922 feature film. It was the first film shot in Technicolor in the United States. Up till then, movies were in black and white. Frances Marion

Anna May Wong in a scene from *The Toll of the Sea*, 1922

wrote the script especially for Anna and based it on the opera *Madama Butterfly*. The story told of a young Chinese woman who finds a white man floating in the sea and falls in love with him, but their interracial romance ends tragically. The movie and Anna were a hit. The *New York Times* praised her as "completely unconscious of the camera," and wrote, "She should be seen again and often on the screen."

Anna worked steadily from then on but was cast only in stereotypical supporting roles as the "demure butterfly" or the cunning villainess. The main Asian characters in movies were played by white actors in "yellowface" makeup. The production code forbade non-white actresses from having romances with white actors. "No film lovers can ever marry me [on-screen]," said Anna. "I must always die in the movies, so that the white girl with the yellow hair may get the man."

Yet Anna attracted attention. Hollywood superstar Douglas Fairbanks spotted her in *The Toll of the Sea* and thought she was sensational. He wanted to cast her as a Mongol servant in his new movie *The Thief of Bagdad* (1924). But first, he had to write to her father and ask permission to hire her. Although the role required that Wong wear a skimpy two-piece costume, her father agreed. He realized that she could earn a great deal of money in films.

The film was an epic fantasy adventure that showcased Fairbanks's gymnastics and charm. When the movie opened at the Liberty Theater in New York on March 18, 1924, incense perfumed the air, and ushers dressed in Arabian costumes served Turkish coffee to ladies in the audience. The film was a smash. The *New York Times* called it an "entrancing picture." *Film Daily* praised

Douglas Fairbanks thrusts a knife into Anna May Wong's
back in *The Thief of Bagdad*, 1924.

Fairbanks, and the two other leads, and singled out Anna as
"good." Critics applauded her self-confidence on the screen, and
the intelligence she portrayed, as well as her beauty. "Anna May is
pure delight," wrote the *San Francisco Chronicle*.

In spite of the national and international success of the film, Anna's
parents were still unhappy with her career choice. "A good girl will not
be an actress," they said. At nineteen, Anna moved out of the family
home and into her own apartment. Unfortunately, she was offered only
small roles. "There are not many Chinese parts," she said.

Out of money, Anna returned to her parents' house. By 1927, she had appeared in more than twenty films but was fed up with the types of roles she had to play.

Her luck changed when German director Richard Eichberg remembered her in *The Thief of Bagdad* and offered her a five-picture contract. She gladly accepted. Anna and Lulu left for Europe. Anna starred as a biracial dancer in Eichberg's 1928 movie *Song.* The film was subtitled in many languages so that it could be seen throughout Europe as well as South Africa and Australia. Anna caused a sensation. As a stunning Chinese American movie actress, she symbolized the modern woman. Journalists interviewed her. Photographers took her picture. German critics wrote, "Anna May Wong is ours now and we won't let her go."

The movie marked a turning point in her life and made her an international star. For her next film, the 1929 *Piccadilly*, shot in London, she wore the latest styles and displayed her talent as a model. Back in Berlin, she dressed in Parisian creations for *Pavement Butterfly.* Everyone wanted to meet her, and she was invited to parties with famous artists and writers. She took her work seriously and studied German for her first talkie, *Flame of Love*, in 1930. Anna mastered the language so well that critics said, "her German is too perfect. She must have had a double."

Despite her success, Anna was homesick. She and Lulu sailed across the Atlantic, planning a short visit in California before returning to Europe. During the voyage Anna received an offer to be cast in the Broadway play *On the Spot,* as a Chinese woman. Anna accepted the part, and the show was a success. But shortly after the play opened, Anna's mother was hit by a car in Los Angeles and died

Portrait of Anna May Wong in a Chinese gown, undated

from her injuries. Anna didn't go home for the funeral but returned home months later. It is not known exactly why she delayed. She may not have wanted to leave the run of her successful play. It was said that her father and other members of her family were angry that she didn't come to the funeral. But according to another version, her father kept her mother's body in a mausoleum until spring when Anna returned, and he did not hold a grudge against her.

Anna remained in California. Despite her fame, she was still offered only sinister parts. In *Daughter of the Dragon*, she played

Dr. Fu Manchu's evil daughter. Dr. Fu Manchu, a character created by a white writer, typified the worst example of a racist Hollywood Chinese villain. A Swedish American actor in yellowface performed the lead. Anna said, "Why is it that the screen Chinese is nearly always the villain of the piece, and so cruel? We are not like that. We have our own virtues. We have our rigid code of behavior, of honor."

By 1931, *Screenplay* magazine reported that Anna planned to return to Europe to get the kind of parts she wanted. But suddenly, Hollywood offered her a better role in *Shanghai Express*, playing opposite a friend from Berlin, actress Marlene Dietrich. The 1932 movie, set in China, became a box office hit and was nominated for Best Picture.

When MGM was ready to film Pearl S. Buck's 1931 novel *The Good Earth*, Anna had read the book and lobbied for what would be the role of a lifetime: O-Lan, the female lead. The story told of poor Chinese farmers struggling to survive over the years. Buck intended that the movie be cast with all Chinese or Chinese American actors. Anna longed to play O-Lan and went for many screen tests. The press supported her as the best choice. However, the studio wanted actor Paul Muni, a Caucasian, for the male lead, Wang Lung, and studio censorship prohibited any interracial on-screen romance. Instead, the part of O-Lan went to Luise Rainer, a German-born actress. Anna was bitterly disappointed. And when MGM offered her the part of a pretty young dancer who lures Wang Lung away from his wife, Anna was outraged. "You're asking me—with Chinese blood—to do the only unsympathetic role in the picture, featuring an all-American cast portraying Chinese characters," she snapped, and turned them down.

Leaving America behind, she traveled to China to discover the "real Chinese" in preparation for her next movie, *Daughter of Shanghai* (1937). Now she wanted to fully embrace her heritage. "For a year I shall study the land of my fathers," she told reporters. "All I knew of the Orient was what my father told me." In Shanghai, she was mobbed by journalists and fans. People everywhere knew her from her movies, billboards, and ads. "This tumultuous greeting from my own people touched me more than anything that ever has happened to me in my motion picture career," said Anna.

At parties she met society and political leaders and members of the film industry. But at a banquet in Nanking, government officials criticized her demeaning portrayals of Chinese women. Anna explained that she didn't write the scripts. To get established in her profession, she could not choose the parts. Anna told them she had come to China to learn more about Chinese women. "I hoped I would be able to interpret our country in a better light," she said. And the critics apologized to her.

In Hong Kong, she joined her father who had returned to China to live with his first wife, and they traveled to his ancestral home. Villagers treated her like a goddess. "Many women could not believe I really existed," said Anna. "They had seen me on the screen, but they thought I was simply a picture invented by a machine!"

By the end of the trip, Anna had found an inner happiness. "A rhythm in the life there harmonized with something in me that had been out of tune," she told a journalist. "I was no longer restless. It's hard to explain—our Chinese expression 'being in harmony with heaven and earth'—is the essence of it." She gave up her stylish Western wardrobe and wore Chinese gowns handmade for her with antique silk.

When she returned to Hollywood, she entered into her most productive period in movies as well as television. She signed a contract with Paramount and designer Edith Head created marvelous costumes for her. Paramount loaned her to Warner Brothers to film *When Were You Born?,* and she played the part of an astrologer who solves crimes. Anna played another amateur Chinese detective in the 1951 television series *The Gallery of Madame Liu-Tsong*, which filmed in New York, and she was a featured guest on many TV shows.

Although Anna never won the type of roles that she truly desired, her sixty-one films opened the way for other Asian American actresses. Nancy Kwan, who starred in *The World of Suzie Wong* in 1960, said that Anna was her role model. Anna was supposed to costar with Kwan in the 1961 musical *Flower Drum Song,* the first all–Asian American film made by a major studio. But before they started shooting, Anna began suffering from recurring liver disease. On February 3, 1961, she died of a heart attack. She was fifty-six. During her lifetime and remarkable career, Anna had won a place as the first Asian American film star.

Anna May Wong had been awarded a star on the Hollywood Walk of Fame in 1960, and in 2019, when Lucy Liu, a film and television actress, became the second Asian American actress to receive a star, she paid tribute to Wong. "I was lucky that trailblazers like Anna May Wong . . . came before me," said Liu. "A hundred years ago, she was a pioneer while enduring racism. If my body of work somehow helped bridge the gap between stereotypical roles, first given to Anna May, and mainstream success today, I am thrilled to have been part of that process."

Director Dorothy Arzner on the set of *Fashions for Women* with actress Esther Ralston, on the left, behind the camera, 1927

CHAPTER 9   DOROTHY ARZNER

"I WANTED TO STAND UP AS A DIRECTOR AND NOT HAVE PEOPLE MAKE ALLOWANCES THAT IT WAS A WOMAN."   —Dorothy Arzner

Dorothy Emma Arzner was not the first female film director in Hollywood. There were dozens of others before her, but she was the most successful. The press often compared Dorothy to the well-known male directors, Cecil B. DeMille and D. W. Griffith. In all, Dorothy directed sixteen movies primarily focused on women's situations—their feelings, friendships, and goals—and her movies have endured.

Born on January 3, 1897, in San Francisco, Dorothy grew up in Hollywood, where her upper-middle-class parents had moved after the 1906 earthquake. Her mother, Jenetter Young Arzner, stayed home to take care of the family. Her father, Louis Arzner, managed the Hoffman Café, a famous restaurant. Movie stars, such as Charlie Chaplin and Mary Pickford, and directors, such as, D. W. Griffith and James Cruze, ate there.

These celebrities sat in a private alcove concealed by a velvet drape. Little Dorothy would peek through a slit in the curtain—to the amusement of Cruze, who introduced her to everybody at the table. Supposedly she went there every day to listen to them talk about acting, writing, and directing. Dorothy later said that although she was around movie actors and directors at her dad's restaurant, they did not influence her choice of career. "I had no personal interest in actors because they were too familiar to me," she recalled.

Dorothy attended Westlake, a private girls' school, from which she graduated in 1915. Although she wore a lacy white dress for her graduation picture, she liked dressing up in boys' clothes and sometimes called herself Garth. She enrolled at the University of Southern California intending to become a doctor, but—despite her good grades—she left after two years. The United States had entered World War I, and Dorothy wanted to become an ambulance driver. Hoping to go to France, she volunteered for the Red Cross ambulance corps but was too young. Instead, she applied for an emergency drivers' unit in Los Angeles led by an army commander.

After the war, Dorothy didn't want to go back to school and wondered what to do. The commander's wife loved motion pictures and said she thought that would be a good business for a young woman like Dorothy. She set up an appointment for Dorothy with William C. DeMille, a screenwriter and director at Paramount Studios. The Spanish flu epidemic, raging at that time, had claimed many lives. So the film industry desperately needed workers. "It was possible for even inexperienced people to have an opportunity if they showed signs of ability or knowledge," recalled Dorothy.

She told DeMille that she wanted a job in the movies. He asked her where she wanted to start, and she said dressing sets. But when he asked her to identify the periods of furniture in his office, she failed, so he suggested she look around the different departments at the studio. Dorothy was particularly impressed with his brother, director Cecil B. DeMille. "If one was going to be in this movie business," she realized, "one should be a director because he was the one who told everyone else what to do." William DeMille's secretary explained to Dorothy that movies began with typing the stories. When Dorothy met with DeMille again and he asked her where she would like to start, she said, "At the bottom."

And he gave her the job of typing scripts. But she was ambitious and wanted to move up. Three months later, she worked as a script supervisor on the movie *Stronger than Death* (1920). Dorothy checked to see where the camera stopped and made sure the actors wore the same clothes each time the scene was shot. She became interested in editing as she watched cutter Nan Heron work on a reel for a picture. Cutters would take a long strip of celluloid film that had been shot, hold it in their hands, view it frame by frame, decide where to cut to best tell the story, then join the pieces together to make a finished picture. Heron let her do the second reel, and Dorothy finished the whole movie. "A good cutter is also an editor," said Dorothy. She would hold the film up to the light and cut it by hand. Dorothy held the film at arm's length and judged the pace that would show on the screen. She cut and spliced thousands of feet of film to create sequences. Soon she became a chief editor and cut and edited fifty-two films. "I worked most of the day and night," she said, "and loved it."

At age twenty-five, she worked on *Blood and Sand,* a 1922 movie starring Rudolph Valentino as a matador. Dorothy efficiently combined stock footage of bullfights with shots of a bullfight she had filmed at a nearby ranch to save money. Director James Cruze, who had known her at her father's restaurant, watched her do the final editing and was astounded. He asked her to cut his next film, *The Covered Wagon* (1923), a historical epic, which she did at night while working on continuity during the day. Dorothy had to make sure that all the details were the same from shot to shot and scene to scene. She also worked with Cruze on *Old Ironsides*, a 1926 adventure of a boy on a merchant ship at sea that is captured by pirates. Fortunately, the USS *Constitution*—nicknamed "Old Ironsides" because of its perfect battle record in the War of 1812—rescues the ship. Dorothy was one of a few women among 3,000 men staying on the *Llewellyn J. Morse*, the square-rig sailing vessel where the movie was filmed. "There was nothing more thrilling than being on that boat in full sail," she recalled. "It was dangerous at every minute."

The cutter was usually on the set with the director and lined up the scenes to shoot. The experience made her feel ready to accept an offer from Columbia Studios to write and direct a silent movie. However, the executives at Paramount wanted her to stay and do a B picture, a cheesy low-budget film that would be a less important feature. They promised to eventually give her a chance to direct a major film. Dorothy demanded that unless she was on a set in two weeks with a big-budget A picture, she'd go to Columbia. "I'd rather do a picture for a small company and have my own way than a B movie for Paramount," she said. The studio boss gave in, and two weeks later Arzner began directing her first feature silent film, *Fashions for Women* (1927).

The movie told of a cigarette girl who sells tobacco and also snacks in a nightclub, and was played by Esther Ralston, star of *Old Ironsides*. She pretends to be a famous fashion model and falls in love with a duke. Although the star and the film received mixed reviews, the press gave Dorothy top billing as "Paramount's first woman director." Critic Brooks Atkinson wrote, "If fashion pictures must be made, let Dorothy Arzner make them." The movie was a commercial success, so Dorothy signed a long-term contract.

Her next film, *Ten Modern Commandments* (1927), also starred Esther Ralston, who had appeared in both *Fashions for Women* and *Old Ironsides*. In this movie the actress portrayed a maid who falls in love with an aspiring songwriter. Critics gave Dorothy credit for doing "what her men directorial rivals had failed to do." Because of Dorothy's ability to bring out Ralston's humor and charm, she soon became known as a "star-maker."

Dorothy also became known for her masculine style of dressing. On the set she usually wore a tailored suit, shirt, and tie. With her short hair brushed back from her forehead, she sometimes wore a felt hat to shade her eyes. A journalist quoted her as saying, that this was "the only sort of costume suitable to her job."

While working on *Ten Modern Commandments*, Dorothy met Marion Morgan, a choreographer who had founded her own troupe and a dance school. Marion, ten years older than Dorothy, had created dances for the film. Marion had also staged a fashion show in *Fashions for Women* and they met on set. Dorothy and Marion became lovers, and were lifelong companions and artistic partners, and soon moved into a home in the Hollywood Hills.

In 1929, Dorothy directed her first talkie, *The Wild Party* starring Clara Bow, who became known as the It Girl. Bow earned the title after starring in *It*, a 1927 romantic comedy. She was the ultimate flapper—a confident, modern young woman of the 1920s who loved to party.

In Dorothy's movie, Bow played the role of a popular student at an all-female college who helps a classmate win a scholarship as

Dorothy Arzner reads a script, 1930s.

well as a boyfriend. The bond between the two women is one of the main themes of the film. This was Bow's first talkie, and she was nervous about her Brooklyn accent. Also the microphones were awkwardly hidden in the furniture, so she couldn't move freely while speaking her lines. Dorothy came up with a brilliant idea. She asked her crew to attach a microphone to the end of a fishing rod and dangle it above Bow as she moved around. Dorothy had invented the first boom microphone!

Dorothy's *next* film, *Sarah and Son* (1930), was hailed as a woman's movie made by women. Even the editor and production assistant were female. In life, as in her films, Dorothy stressed the importance of the community of women. For this movie and more that followed, Dorothy collaborated with screenwriter Zoe Akins, whose work she greatly respected. "No director will have a good script or a good picture unless he has a good writer," said Dorothy. "I bow to a writer at all times. In fact, I have tried to always keep a writer on the set with me."

Dorothy's heroines reflected her own spirit of independence. In the 1933 movie *Christopher Strong*, Katharine Hepburn starred as an aviatrix who falls in love with a married member of Parliament. It was Hepburn's second film. Dorothy chose her when she spotted her at the studio filming a movie set in a jungle. Hepburn "was up a tree with a leopard skin on!" recalled Dorothy. "Talking to her, I felt she was the very modern type I wanted for *Christopher Strong*." In the movie, Hepburn wore a tomboy outfit: jodhpurs (English horse-riding pants), a tailored jacket, and a beanie. At the end of the movie, she gives up her love affair and her life by breaking the world altitude record, whipping off her oxygen mask, and letting her plane nosedive.

Dorothy Arzner poses with equipment, 1930s.

Some people thought that the flying scenes were inspired by Amelia Earhart's flight across the Atlantic in 1932. Dorothy, however, insisted that the British aviation pioneer Amy Johnson who flew solo from London to Australia in 1930, was the model for her character. Later Dorothy said, "*Christopher Strong* was one of the favorites of my pictures at the time."

Dorothy's most famous movie, *Dance, Girl, Dance*, in 1940, starred newcomers Lucille Ball and Maureen O'Hara as chorus girl buddies. Judy (Maureen O'Hara) longs to dance ballet, but to earn a living, she does a hula dance audition for the manager of a burlesque club. Bubbles (Lucille Ball) arrives late for the audition and flirts with the manager so, of course, gets the job. She persuades the club to hire Judy to do a ballet solo as an opening number. The audience consists mainly of sleazy men who heckle Judy until Bubbles comes on in a slinky gown. At a climactic moment, Judy charges to the edge of the stage and angrily scolds the men for ogling her and Bubbles. A woman in the audience— who works at the ballet company that Judy hopes to join—rises and claps her hands in support of Judy, and slowly the rest of the crowd stands and applauds.

Dorothy rewrote the script to highlight the contrast between Judy's sensitive artistic goals, and Bubbles's hardboiled desire for money. In the 1970s when women campaigned for equal rights and equal opportunities, they embraced Dorothy's movie for expressing their views. Feminist critics were delighted "to find a woman director among all of the men in Hollywood film history." The film is still considered a work of major importance.

Dorothy was the first female member of the Directors Guild

Joseph Walker on the left, and Dorothy Arzner peer
through the camera lens during production of an
unidentified film, about 1943.

of America, and the guild paid tribute to her in 1975. When
interviewed Dorothy said, "I was so averse to having any comment
made about being a woman director, that in my first contract I
asked that I didn't even have screen credit on the picture because
I wanted to stand up as a director and not have people make
allowances that it was a woman."

In Dorothy's later years, she taught at the UCLA Film School.
One of her students was Francis Ford Coppola, who went on

to write and direct *The Godfather* trilogy. "She wasn't teaching because she needed a job," recalled Coppola. "She was teaching because she loved the movies so much." He said that Miss Arzner had "an enormous heart" and would bring boxes of crackers and cookies to class because she knew how many of her students, like Coppola, had little money. "There was a lot of wisdom that Miss Arzner had picked up over a long career as a professional," he said. "One thing she told me that I have in fact told my children [directors Sofia and Roman], she said always sit in the same place right next to the camera because it's the best view of what the performers are doing." The director could also look up at the cameraman's face and tell from his expression if the scene had gone right. But most of all, the actors could see the director. "They're doing it for you," said Coppola. "As Miss Arzner told me, after all, what is a director more than just a coach to support the actors?"

During a low period, Coppola was so broke he considered dropping out of film school and getting a job as a stage manager, but Miss Arzner stopped to talk to him after class, and gave him the leftover box of cookies for dinner. She said to him, "You'll make it. I know." And that "crumb of encouragement" inspired him to stay at UCLA, finish the program, and pursue a film career.

Dorothy remembered being a young pioneer herself, striving for independence as she struggled to achieve her goal. She said, "To be a director you cannot be subject to anyone, even the head of the studio. I threatened to quit each time I didn't get my way, but no one ever let me walk out."

Margaret Booth at her desk editing film, about 1930s

CHAPTER 10 MARGARET BOOTH

"IN THE SILENT DAYS, YOU LEARNED ABOUT RHYTHM, AND YOU
LEARNED TO CUT FILM LIKE POETRY." —Margaret Booth

Margaret Booth said she was the first person—female or male—to be given the title of film editor. At the beginning of her long career, few paid attention to the cutters and joiners like Margaret who decided where to cut the celluloid film, and literally join the pieces with tape or glue to make a finished picture. In those early days, the silent movie was simply a series of tiny photographs strung together in a sequence and projected over a light source to create the illusion of movement. Margaret was amazed when she began her career. "When I saw a film on the screen," she said, "I thought that's how it came out of the camera. I had no idea how it was put together."

As a girl she loved movies and recalled that she and her mother, also named Margaret, "went to every picture that was playing." Margaret was born on January 16, 1898, and grew up in Los Angeles. Her older brother Elmer was an actor on the New York stage, and Director D. W. Griffith had brought him to California to perform in his films. He played the part of the Gish sisters' older brother in their very first movie for Griffith, *An Unseen Enemy*, in 1912. Three years later Elmer died in a tragic accident when the car his friend was driving crashed into a train hurtling down the tracks in Los Angeles. Griffith delivered the eulogy at the graveside.

Shortly after, he offered Margaret a job as a film joiner to help pay the family bills. She was seventeen and accepted the position. As soon as she graduated from high school, she went to work, but she "didn't know what that work meant." In the laboratory, Margaret and other young women joiners assembled rolls of celluloid film into thousand-foot reels.

Margaret quickly caught on to the task and was soon promoted to the job of negative cutter. The negative was difficult to work with since what appeared light would be dark when printed and was used to make the final copy of the film. Griffith was a genius at alternating long shots, medium shots, and close-ups to create tension and to shape the story. He would project the film and say how he wanted the scene to go. Back in the lab, Margaret learned how to cut negatives by eye, often squinting through a magnifying glass. Since she couldn't watch the film as she was working on it, she had to quickly pull the negative through her fingers, figure out where to cut with scissors, and glue the pieces together. "It was very tedious work," she recalled.

When Griffith closed his Los Angeles studio in 1919 and moved his production company to New York, Margaret stayed in California and found a job at Louis B. Mayer's studio. There she worked with director John Stahl and became his assistant. She would go to the projection room with him to see his dailies (material shot that day) and watch while he cut. She closely studied his methods. He would tell her *why* he wanted a close-up in a particular spot of the movie—a line mouthed by a character in a long shot (from a distance), could be emphasized and given "greater importance" by adding a close-up. "He taught me the dramatic values of cutting," said Margaret, "he taught me about tempo—in fact, he taught me how to edit." Stahl was a perfectionist and would shoot a scene five times, print all the "takes" (scenes photographed without an interruption), then cut the film in different ways. At night Margaret would go back to the projection room and experiment with the film Stahl had left on the cutting-room floor. She stayed till two or three in the morning using the outtakes. "I was practicing cutting with them," she said, "learning to do it on my own." Stahl knew what she was up to. One day he couldn't get a sequence the way he wanted it and asked Margaret, "Did you cut this at all, with the outtakes, at night?"

"Yes," she admitted, "but was frightened to show it to him." He took her footage, liked it better than his own, and used it in the final movie. From then on, she began to edit his films. "I used to count to get the rhythm. I would count as if I were counting music, to give the scene the right tempo. When you worked in the silent days, you learned about rhythm, and you learned to cut film like poetry," Margaret said. She understood that directors used a definite beat in their movies, and it was the cutter's job to bring it out in the editing. That's what made a "good picture." Stahl gave her screen credit for her work on *The Dangerous Age*, a 1923 silent film, but she insisted that he "was really the cutter."

A year later Mayer merged with Metro Pictures to form MGM on the old Goldwyn lot in Culver City. Now there were too many movies under production for Margaret to assist only Stahl. Over the next few years, she cut silent films for a number of directors and said, "I enjoyed working for everyone." Yet Stahl asked her to go with him when he left to establish an independent studio. She preferred staying at MGM. "I knew everybody there," she said, "and never wanted to work any other place. MGM was like home to me. It was really a great family studio." She was twenty-six.

In 1929, she was cutting *The Bridge of San Luis Rey,* which started out as a silent movie but then became a "part-talkie." Making films with sound was a challenge. "We were all new at it," she said, "and I thought it was terrifying." Margaret had to add a talking sequence—a thin celluloid strip printed with recorded sound—at the beginning and end of the film, and get it synchronized to match the images. "At first I was so frightened . . . that it wasn't going to be in sync," she recalled. She ran the picture in the sound department for the technicians from RCA's radio company and felt annoyed to have "electronic people" watching the film with her, especially when they found one frame uncoordinated. Up till then she and the editors could "throw the film around in any way."

When Irving Thalberg, dubbed "the boy wonder," became head of MGM's production in 1924, things changed for Margaret. Young, brilliant, and enthusiastic, he had an amazing instinct for what the public wanted, and a gift for storytelling. He noticed Margaret's talent. She recognized his and said, "he was the greatest man who was ever in pictures." Thalberg supervised over forty films a year at MGM, from selecting the scripts to approving the final editing. Margaret sat beside him at the screenings of previews so they could discuss ideas and make possible changes. He would turn to her and say, "How do you feel about that as a woman?"

Sometimes, if Thalberg felt a film was in trouble, he decided to preview an uncut print the next night on a big screen at a theater. If the audience laughed at something that was supposed to be dramatic, it was changed. "It was easier to fix things in those days," recalled Margaret. "You could run down to the stage . . . and say, 'I need a close-up.'" The cameraman was under contract and still there, ready to help her. Once she edited and reedited a movie in a single day, then rushed to deliver the footage to a theater for a preview. Thalberg applauded her and assigned her to cut the studio's biggest movies.

In 1935, she worked on *Mutiny on the Bounty* starring Clark Gable and Charles Laughton. The adventure, set in the eighteenth century, told of the brutal Captain Bligh (Laughton) of the ship HMS *Bounty*, who mistreats his crew on a voyage to Tahiti. The first mate Fletcher Christian (Gable) disapproves of the captain's behavior and, on their trip home, leads the crew in a revolt. The mutineers seize control of the ship and set Captain Bligh adrift on the high seas.

At the beginning of production, the film's director took a unit of cameramen to Tahiti to shoot the exteriors and brought the footage back to the studio. As Margaret edited the movie, she said, "Every time I needed a piece from Tahiti, I just went to the bin and there it was. It was all lined up before they even started shooting here." Scenes of the boat on the open sea were shot near Catalina Island, off the coast of Los Angeles. "Catalina was the base of operations," said Margaret. "I used to fly to Catalina every day with the film and view it with the director, . . . and then come back and cut it." When the completed movie was previewed at a theater in Santa Barbara, it got a standing ovation. "It was wonderful," remembered Margaret. *Mutiny* was a huge box office success. The *New York Times* wrote that it was "savagely exciting and rousingly dramatic." *Variety* called it, "Hollywood at its very best."

Camera crew and cast of *Mutiny on the Bounty* on location
at Catalina Island, 1935

Thalberg recognized the importance of Margaret's achievement
and thought that the title of "cutter" didn't give her enough credit.
So he credited her on the screen with the title "film editor." Soon
the entire industry adopted the term. In 1935, the Academy of
Motion Picture Arts and Sciences introduced a Best Film Editing
category for the Academy Awards. Margaret was nominated for
editing *Mutiny*. Although she didn't win, the movie received an
Oscar for Best Picture. Later when asked which of the films she

edited she was most proud of, she said, "The picture I liked most of all was *Mutiny on the Bounty.*"

The following year she and Thalberg collaborated on Shakespeare's *Romeo and Juliet* starring Leslie Howard and Thalberg's wife Norma Shearer. Because Thalberg demanded perfection, Margaret had to review and edit five versions of the balcony scene shot from different camera positions.

Leslie Howard, as Romeo, holds the hand of Norma Shearer, as Juliet, in *Romeo and Juliet*, 1936.

The last picture she did with Thalberg was *Camille* starring Greta Garbo. "It's a gorgeous picture to see," said Margaret. While she was cutting it, Thalberg asked her to direct movies. Margaret refused. "I enjoyed what I was doing," she said, and told him, "I want to be the best, if I can, at that."

While *Camille* was still in production, Thalberg died suddenly of pneumonia. He had suffered from health problems since childhood. Some people left, but Margaret stayed on. A year later, Mayer promoted her to the role of supervising editor where she controlled the dailies of every film the studio made. Margaret worked on the first movie that MGM produced overseas in England, *A Yank at Oxford*. "I was the cutter on it," she said, "and Mr. Mayer sent my mother and me over. We had never been abroad before, and it was a lovely trip." A great deal of the film was shot outdoors, including a boat race on the River Thames.

From then on, Margaret never went back to the cutting room to physically do the first steps of the process. "Directors and editors work on a picture," she said, "and then I come in and finish it." In the projection room, she approved the final editing of sound, images, visual effects, and length, and had the power to order reshoots. No film left MGM without her consent. Margaret oversaw classics such as *The Wizard of Oz*, starring Judy Garland. For her, editing a musical was "quite different."

"You have to know when to cut on the downbeats [the first beats in a measure of music]. . . . Of course, I feel that way about any editing. It has to be done rhythmically."

Margaret held her position at MGM till 1968 when she was seventy years old. Dedicated to her work, she never married.

When asked about her personal life she said, "I don't think there's very much to tell." In 1978 she received an honorary Oscar for her contribution to film and said, "Isn't it wonderful that one can win an award for something one loves to do?"

Film editor Thelma Schoonmaker felt the same way about their profession. In 2007, Thelma won her third Oscar for *The Departed* and admitted "I think I have the best job in the world, taking unshaped footage and making a story out of it." Perhaps referring to Margaret, she said, "There were women editors way back in the early days, and there are many many women film editors today.

"We don't make movies for awards. We have the most wonderful reward, which is the reaction of our friends and the audience."

Portrait of Clare West by photographer Eugene Robert
Richee, about 1923

CHAPTER 11 CLARE WEST

"THE SCREEN DOES NOT FOLLOW ANY STYLE—IT *IS* THE STYLE!."

—Clare West

Clare West was among the first to officially hold the title of costume designer in film. A hundred years ago, she was well known as she introduced new styles on the screen. She adored fashion and designed her own beautifully tailored clothes. Photos of her sketching or meeting with directors show her wearing elegant dresses with little or no jewelry. Clare was a trendsetter on and off the screen.

When she began her career at Triangle Studio in 1914 for silent film director D. W. Griffith, there were no costume departments. Actors and actresses wore their own everyday clothes. Clever actresses who came to auditions dressed for the part usually got the roles. The others chose outfits from a rack of secondhand or rented clothes in a department called "wardrobe." So Clare began her work in film as "head of wardrobe."

Clare West was supposedly born on January 30, 1893, in Clinton, Missouri. As a child she made clothes for each of her dolls "to suit its particular personality," and imagined the "great occasion" when they would be wearing the outfits. She revealed that she "always loved clothes and had been professionally designing since her early teens. . . . I had definite intentions of making clothes my career!"

It is not clear how Clare got her start. A film historian believes

Clare was already selling her sketches to women's magazines while she was still in high school. After graduating from college in the 1910s, she studied fashion illustration in Paris, and became a successful fashion artist. Clare told a reporter that she had learned "costume design wherever best teachers of this subject were obtainable." By 1916, at the age twenty-three, *Motion Picture News* reported that "Madame Clare West . . . who received her training in Paris, has been placed in charge of the costume department of the Fine Arts studio," that was owned by Triangle, Griffith's company.

In other accounts Clare was working as a seamstress in Los Angeles when Griffith hired her to design the women's costumes for *The Birth of a Nation*. She had to find out what ladies wore at the time and make the clothes attractive on the one hand, and on the other, seem lived in. Clare proved to be a wonderful researcher, combining historical accuracy with a sense of what would appeal to modern audiences.

When she completed costumes for Griffith's 1916 film *Intolerance: Love's Struggle Throughout the Ages*, he promoted her to the position of "studio designer." It was the first movie to feature elaborate costumes for sixty-three cast members plus more than 3,000 extras. For this picture," Clare said, "I had the unusual experience of having to make duplicates, and even triplicates of practically every garment." The rehearsals and screening took two years and the clothes got "worn over and over again . . . and lost their freshness."

Intolerance consisted of four parallel stories set in different historic periods, ending in contemporary times. The first story took place in Babylon in 539 BCE. The second told of the last days of Christ.

Seena Owen in Babylonian costume designed by Clare
West for *Intolerance*, 1916

The third depicted the massacre of French Protestants in 1572. And the fourth, a "modern" story, told of a conflict between striking workers and the owners of a mill. Clare collaborated with French artist Paul Iribe.

Clare and Iribe worked well together. The costumes they designed sparked a fashion trend in America. The April 1917 issue of *Photoplay* magazine featured an article titled "Back to Babylon for New Fashions," and included sketches for women to copy and sew at home. Since most women moviegoers couldn't travel to France—or even dream of going to Paris, much less Babylon—they flocked to the movies for fashion ideas. Clare's costumes had to anticipate a look that would still be chic by the time the movie got released months or even a year later.

Director Cecil B. DeMille understood women's desire for "larger than life clothing," and realized that this was a way to lure them into the theater. Impressed by Clare's work on *Intolerance*, he hired her in 1918 to produce costumes for ten movies at his company Famous Players-Lasky, which later became Paramount. DeMille told her, "I want clothes that will make people gasp when they see them . . . don't design anything anybody could possibly buy in a store."

And she didn't. For the 1920 comedy *Why Change Your Wife?*, starring Gloria Swanson, she designed outfits that transformed the heroine from an ordinary housewife into a 1920s fashion plate. The whole plot hinged on the costumes. Clare produced six sleeveless, backless gowns for Swanson that made the star look glamorous. Swanson said that performing in DeMille's movie was like "playing house in the world's most expensive department store," complete with real jewelry. Clare was asked if stars like

Chariot outside the Babylonian Gate in a scene from
Intolerance, 1916

Swanson were ever cranky and refused to wear gowns that she had
made for them. She replied, "I have never yet designed for any
actress who was not perfectly content to leave the dressing entirely
to me." She added, "You must please an actress with the things
you give her to wear."

In *The Affairs of Anatole* (1921), Bebe Daniels was pleased to
model Clare's famous "octopus gown" and sheer cape. Clare had
obviously studied drawings and photos of octopuses, and perhaps

Bebe Daniels wears the octopus gown designed by Clare West in a scene from *The Affairs of Anatole*, 1921.

the real thing, for this elaborate garment. Her color sketches for the costumes were featured in the August 1921 issue of *Motion Picture* magazine along with photos of actresses wearing the gowns. "I try to have the clothes symbolic of the character," said Clare. In this movie, Daniels played "the wickedest woman in New York," so she appropriately wore a gown resembling a "devil fish . . . dangerous to men." Clare's costumes came *before* the scenarist wrote the script, to help her get the right "feel" for the movie.

Color mattered, too. Although the films were seen in black, white, and gray, Clare said that color value had to be carefully studied. "One must know exactly how a certain shade will appear when transferred to the screen," she said. She also understood which fabrics and ornaments photographed well.

Clare faced new challenges with each project. For *Adam's Rib,* a 1923 film with a sequence about Ice Age tribes, her attention to details set a standard for Hollywood costumers. Clare made twenty-five fur and leopard skin costumes without stitches since her research led her to believe that sewing was unknown at the time. She also formed jewelry out of real bones, claws, and feathers.

Clare's fellow designer Iribe joined her to work on *The Ten Commandments* for DeMille in 1923. Again Clare relied on research as well as her creativity to produce costumes for the two-part epic film. The Prologue, set in Biblical times, tells of the Exodus of the Israelites from Egypt. Miriam, the sister of Moses, wears a simple robe, but the Pharaoh is adorned with arm ornaments, pendants, and amulets. The second part of the film tells of two modern-day brothers—one religious, and the other, an atheist. For this section, Clare traveled to Paris to see the latest evening gown fashions and

Clare West (right) and director Cecil B. DeMille compare her design sketch to the actual dress, modeled by Pauline Garon, on the set of *Adam's Rib*, 1923.

to buy material. Another member of her team traveled to Egypt, India, and Palestine to gather information. Back at the studio, Clare put together files to help her and more than a hundred seamstresses construct three thousand costumes out of 333,000 yards of cloth.

Fans and movie stars adored her work. She received several hundred letters a day begging her to copy a dress that had been worn in a movie and make it available to the public.

Charles de Rochefort as the Pharaoh in a scene from
The Ten Commandments with costumes designed by
Clare West, 1923

Clare believed that Hollywood led Paris in fashion. For her,
"The screen does not follow any style—it *is* the style!" and "The
American motion picture has become . . . the dictator of the world's
fashions," she claimed. "I am more proud than ever of our own
United States. Our designers, especially those whose work is reflected
on our screen, are months ahead of those of Paris and London." An
article, "Read How Paris Copies Styles Set by Hollywood," in the
March 1925 issue of *Motion Picture* magazine agreed. It revealed that

twenty-two Paris dressmakers were sent to see American movies as inspiration for their haute couture (high fashion).

When Clare designed runway outfits for a fashion show in Paramount's movie *The Dressmaker from Paris*, it was the high point of her career and her last job on a movie. After that she opened her own salon in Los Angeles, and outfitted superstars off screen with her "cutting-edge styles."

"Sometimes," she said, "I make up a gown or suit or wrap in the same style as something which has been worn in a picture." She also designed dresses for Hamburger's, a huge department store in downtown LA. Crowds gathered to view her sketches displayed in the store's windows.

Clare never lost her dedication to the field of costume design. She joined forces with screenwriter Frances Marion, and the three Talmadge sisters (who were leading actresses) to plan a costume museum. Every period in motion picture history would be represented, and the garments kept in glass cases. Although the museum was never built, the idea showed Clare's commitment to preserve and honor her profession's contribution to film.

Perhaps Clare's biggest commitment was establishing the importance of the costume designer in filmmaking. A movie magazine journalist wrote, "Beautiful gowns are as essential to the success of a motion picture as a beautiful heroine."

Clare was entered in the Costume Designer Guild's Hall of Fame in 2003, and many of her creations have been exhibited at the Metropolitan Museum of Art in New York. Hollywood costume designers in recent years seem to have the same work methods as Clare. Ruth E. Carter, who won an Oscar for 2018's *Black Panther*, said, "I find that immersing yourself in research really does give you the heart and soul of what you're doing. . . . Not only am I creating costumes, I'm also creating a story and a mood." For the Afrofuturistic film, Carter studied, and was inspired by, clothing worn by various African peoples. Kids today wear copies of Carter's costumes to dress up as superheroes, just as women wore copies of Clare's costumes a century ago to look like stylish movie stars.

CHAPTER 12 HELEN HOLMES

"IF I WANT THRILLY ACTION, I ASK PERMISSION TO WRITE IT IN
MYSELF."
—Helen Holmes

Every week, female action star Helen Holmes performed daredevil stunts in her silent movie serial *The Hazards of Helen*. She thrilled audiences by leaping to the top of speeding trains, chasing fleeing bandits, and riding a motorcycle off a bridge to catch a runaway train. Helen, the actress and stuntwoman, was not a "damsel in distress." She rescued others with her extraordinary courage and quick thinking. Since so many of her serials showed her jumping on and off moving trains, and preventing train crashes, Helen came to be known as "the Railroad Girl."

Helen, the youngest of three children, was born in South Bend, Indiana, on June 19, 1893, to Louis R. and Sophie Barnes Holmes. Helen grew up around trains. Her father worked for the Illinois Central Railroad, and later for the Chicago and Eastern Illinois. As a girl, she even learned how to drive a train engine. She once told an interviewer that she was born in Chicago, grew up in Sound Bend, and attended the Art Institute of Chicago. And she told another journalist that she modeled for Santa Fe Railroad posters.

But movie magazines tended to exaggerate the facts.

There are also conflicting stories about how she came to Los Angeles. It is believed that when she was around eighteen, her older brother Frank invited her to his ranch in the Funeral Mountains near Death Valley. She loved riding and roping, and she learned how to pan for gold. According to another source, her brother became ill with tuberculosis, and needed to move to the dry, hot climate of Death Valley. All versions agree that when Helen's brother died, she moved to Los Angeles, where in 1912 she met actress Mabel Normand, who introduced her to director Mack Sennett. Sennett was the king of the Fun Factory at Keystone Studios. Known for wild car chases as well as comedies, he gave Holmes a contract to use her "motoring skills," and she appeared in at least eighteen of his silent movies.

Helen loved driving. She had wanted to be a competitive race-car driver, but that career wasn't open to women. At that time, women were fighting for suffrage—the right to vote—and the car symbolized their cause. Suffragists drove to rallies in cars decorated with flowers and "Votes for Women" banners to gain support.

Helen fit right into their campaign. In her off time, she liked to race cars, sometimes entering using only an initial to bypass rules forbidding women competitors. She drove in her films, too. One author describes an episode of *The Girl and the Game* in which "Helen controls the wheel, while her three brawny male buddies are relegated to mere passengers."

Helen Holmes drove cars in Keystone movies in 1912, which gave her the opportunity to drive at top speed and get paid for it. Later she bought her own car. A picture in the January 1916 edition of *Photoplay* magazine shows her behind the wheel of what appears to be a Studebaker Speedster. The caption reads, "Racing-driver Helen Holmes . . . not only drives her own machine, but, clad in pride and overalls, does all the mechanical work that the fast little car may require."

After a year at Keystone, Helen signed a contract with Kalem Studios and met director J. P. (Jack) McGowan, an Australian horse trainer and actor. He too came from a railroad family. McGowan had grown up in a railroad-junction town, and his father had worked on locomotive crews all his life. His grandfather had been a locomotive engine driver in Scotland.

Helen and McGowan fell in love, married, and became creative partners. With their shared interest in trains, most of their movies were railroad dramas. Their backgrounds brought realism and accuracy to the films. Helen was already popular as the Railroad Girl,

Helen Holmes featured in the *Baltimore and Ohio Employees Magazine*, of the B&O Railroad, date unknown

Helen Holmes tied to a train's wheels in a scene from an unidentified production, about 1915.

when she and McGowan started producing her famous serial, *The Hazards of Helen*. She had the idea of writing a scenario about a young woman telegraph operator in a railroad office. "It was my first attempt," she said. "We made the story and shipped it to New York, waiting with fear and trembling for the verdict of the home office," recalled Helen. "Imagine my elation when instructions came back to make a series!" The first of 119 episodes was released on November 14, 1914.

These short films, screened before a main feature, starred Helen in the role she had created. The action stories showed that a woman could do her job in the workplace—*plus* fight crime. Helen had heard that an actual telegrapher had complained that telegraphing in movies looked fake, so she learned how to send and receive messages to make her performance authentic.

Unlike serials such as *The Perils of Pauline*, which had installments ending in cliffhangers "to be continued," each episode of *The Hazards of Helen* told a complete story. "The Escape on the Fast Freight," episode thirteen, opens with the sheriff delivering a cashbox to Helen. Two tramps lock her in a closet, steal the money, and get away. Helen loses her job to a male operator, but she spots the robbers on a train, climbs down a trestle, drops onto the moving train, tackles the thieves, brings them to justice—and wins back her job.

Helen codirected this episode with costar Leo Maloney, who played one of the crooks. Her husband, the usual director, was in the hospital recovering from a fall from a telephone pole while filming a previous episode.

Helen often wrote the scripts. "Nearly all scenario-writers and authors for the films are men," she told a magazine journalist. "And men usually won't provide for a girl things to do that they wouldn't do themselves. So if I want really thrilly action, I ask permission to write it in myself."

There were no rehearsals. Helen didn't know if a stunt she planned would work till she tried it. The dangers she faced in the movies were real. Once she became trapped inside a burning train. Another time she was driving a truck down a steep grade when

Helen Holmes tied to a train's wheels in a scene from an unidentified production, about 1915

the brakes gave out and she crashed. Movie magazines celebrated her bravery. One fan wrote that he was worried about her "dainty figure" throwing itself around the tops of speeding trains. "You'd think a pretty girl like Helen would be afraid of spoiling her looks," wrote Helen's husband, "but nothing worries her."

A 1915 article in *Photoplay* reported that "Helen wears pretty gowns and is very proud of the fact that she can burst the sleeves of any of them by doubling up her biceps."

To prove that she performed the stunts herself, she staged a breathtaking feat at the California State Fair in 1917 on Helen Holmes Day. A train collision was staged in her honor. Two locomotives going forty miles an hour headed toward each other.

Helen Holmes in a scene after saving the life of a driver whose auto crashed into a locomotive

Before a crowd of thousands, Helen jumped from one of the trains into a moving car seconds before the locomotives crashed and became "a mass of twisted steel and iron."

Helen wanted to show that women could be action heroes too. Her strong, independent character inspired female moviegoers to have confidence. She truly represented that "women will be whatever they want," wrote a film scholar.

Helen and McGowan eventually left Kalem Studios to set up their own company, Signal Hill Productions. They produced new serials, *The Girl and the Game* and *A Lass of the Lumberlands*, full of the "thrilly action" that Helen enjoyed. In one episode, she saves her boyfriend and her father from a train disaster, and in another story, she uncouples a freight train to prevent a "terrible wreck."

When Helen adopted a baby girl, Dorothy Holmes McGowan, she soon became part of the action—appearing in *A Lass of the Lumberlands* and in another thriller where she held Helen's hand, forging across a raging river. Although Helen wanted to keep her daughter in overalls, Dorothy grew up to become a glamorous model who preferred silk gowns.

The strain of working intensely at a frantic pace on so many movies affected Helen's marriage. The couple separated, and Helen bought a ranch in Utah, and raised chickens, horses, and goats. She told *Photoplay* that she planned to be a cattle queen someday. In the meantime, the Mutual Film Corporation that had backed their company, Signal Hill, collapsed, and she and McGowan could no longer produce their own movies.

Helen returned to acting a year later, and signed a contract with Warner Brothers, to make serials under her independent company Helen Holmes Productions. Her movie *The Danger Trail* with cowboy star Hoot Gibson came out in 1920. Helen had always loved dogs and trained Irish terriers to be in movies with her. She and one of her terriers appeared with Gibson in *40-Horse Hawkins*, a 1924 comedy. In 1925's *Webs of Steel*, Holmes was up to her old tricks and rescued a child and a puppy trapped on a railroad trestle while wearing high heels.

But adventurous women in serials became less popular in the 1920s. Women had won the vote in March of 1920, and the new image of a modern woman was a fun-loving stylish young girl called a flapper.

Helen still had fans. One of them was a teenager who wanted to become an actor. His name was John Wayne, and he later admitted that he had a crush on Helen. In 1932, McGowan directed Wayne in *The Hurricane Express,* a twelve-part cliffhanger serial with sound—his first major role. Perhaps as a tribute to Helen, Wayne played a pilot who pursues a villain who causes train wrecks.

But by the mid-1930s, the *Los Angeles Times* reported that "there are no more serial queens. . . . the serials now prefer to let their menfolk wear the pants." Short male actors put on dresses and wigs and doubled as stuntmen for the leading ladies. Men had taken over the movie business. It was time for Helen to retire.

A few stuntwomen struggled to get work doubling for the stars despite the lack of opportunities. Later they formed a professional association to gain recognition. "Today's stuntwomen are the direct descendants of these silent movie actresses," wrote a film historian. They admire the work of stars like Helen who not only acted, directed, and owned their companies, but did the dangerous stunts themselves.

As a film critic wrote, "In her day, Helen Holmes was a hero."

AFTERWORD
WOMEN IN HOLLYWOOD TODAY

The women featured in this book truly blazed a trail for other female filmmakers. They were among the firsts in their fields and did everything from acting, writing, and directing, to performing their own stunts. "Women virtually controlled the film industry during the silent film era," wrote a movie historian. Many such as Mary Pickford, Marion Wong, and Helen Holmes even owned and ran their own independent production companies. Low budgets and short films gave them a chance to experiment in front of and behind the camera, and they made up the rules as they went along. "Talent and brains were what mattered, not gender."

But the picture literally changed in the late 1920s as moviemaking became a big moneymaking business. Wall Street invested. Women were victims of their own success as men took over leadership roles and pushed them out. Males formed unions excluding women. Female-owned companies collapsed. But Mary Pickford, a shrewd businesswoman as well as a star, held on to her partnership in United Artists.

Although many directors and editors were forced out of their jobs in the 1930s, Dorothy Arzner and Margaret Booth both kept working because of their enormous talent and ability. Experienced female screenwriters such as Frances Marion also carried on, and she had more freedom to write realistic dialogue for movies with sound. Costume designers were finally recognized for their contribution to film and inspiring fashion trends, just as Clare West had done. An Academy Award for costume design was established in 1948, and Edith Head won the first of her Oscars the following year. Yet, aside from costume designers, fewer women than ever before held leading positions in Hollywood. The problem was partly due to a new form of entertainment, television.

During the 1940s, moviemaking lost money as people stayed home to watch TV. Stars like Lillian Gish and Anna May Wong easily made the transition to TV roles, but in 1955, movie attendance dropped to its lowest level. Mary Pickford and Charlie Chaplin, the last original owners of United Artists, sold their shares of the company. From then on, UA was repeatedly bought and sold, until eventually merging with MGM.

Women struggled to regain their power in Hollywood. "Emulating their sisters from the early days of the industry, women began finding ways to move their desired projects forward by multitasking," wrote a film historian. Once again, women formed their own production companies or became their own screenwriters and acted in their own films.

A breakthrough event occurred in 1980 when Sherry Lansing became president of 20th Century Fox. Like women before her, she had started out as an actress, then as a script reader, story editor, and production assistant, until reaching the peak of her career in 1992, as CEO of Paramount Pictures.

Things were looking up! Fast forward to the 2000s, when Sofia Coppola won an Oscar for Best Original Screenplay in 2003 for *Lost in Translation*, and she was also nominated as Best Director. Her father, director Francis Ford Coppola, had been one of Dorothy Arzner's prize students, and he had passed her legendary teachings on to his daughter.

Yet women continue to fight for equality in Hollywood. "Today women behind the camera are . . . under represented," said film scholar Cari Beauchamp. "Discrimination against women exists," said director Maria Giese. The Center for the Study of Women in Television & Film, headed by Dr. Martha M. Lauzen at San Diego State University, tracks the numbers of women on the set. Although 50 percent of the movie audience consists of women, men outnumber them two to one as major characters and in speaking roles in films. The Center's *Celluloid Ceiling Report* found that, in 2021, women directed 17 percent of the 250 top-grossing films, 17 percent were writers, 22 percent were editors, and only 6 percent were cinematographers. However, when a film has at least one female director, more women are cast as lead characters and hired for behind-the-scenes jobs.

Diversity poses another challenge. More than half the leading characters in films produced in 2021 were white, 16.4 percent were Black, 12.8 percent were Latino, and 10 percent were Asian.

Ava DuVernay, a Black filmmaker and creator of television shows, founded the production company Array, dedicated to gender and racial inclusion. She notes that Asian Americans have had almost no representation in film and TV, and says, "We can do so much better."

The good news is that Chinese-born Chloe Zhao became the second female director to win an Oscar in 2021. Her movie *Nomadland*, starring Frances McDormand, also won an Oscar for Best Picture. In March 2022, Jane Campion became the third woman to win an Oscar as Best Director for *The Power of the Dog*.

"The future is female," cheered a film historian.

Women in the film industry today can be just as powerful as the pioneers who blazed the trail and built Hollywood.

HONORING ANNA MAY WONG

The US Mint honored trailblazer Anna May Wong by featuring her face on the quarter. The coin, part of the American Women Quarters Program, was released on October 25, 2022.

AUTHOR'S NOTE

Growing up in the Bronx, before we had television, I loved movies and still do. Double features at our neighborhood theater were a Saturday night tradition for my parents and me. Of course, although I was chubby and flat-footed, I wanted to be an actress when I grew up. But I did have curly hair. Later I was amazed to read that stars of the silent films, such as Mary Pickford, were exactly my height, five feet, and had curls, and were therefore able to play the roles of little girls and teenagers when they were adults. Intrigued, I thought of writing a book called *Girls with Curls: Stars of the Silver Screen*. But my editor suggested expanding the idea to write about the women who worked in various branches of the early movie industry—writers, directors, editors, even stuntwomen!

There were many fascinating people to consider as subjects. I chose twelve who were acknowledged as "firsts" in their fields and paved the way for others. Diversity was a theme I wanted to emphasize, and I looked for women of color and different ethnicities. I was astounded to discover Marion Wong, the first Chinese American to establish her own film company and produce a movie about Chinese Americans. And Louise Beavers, who not only starred in the first major role for a Black actress but was also a civil rights activist here in Los Angeles.

Along the way, I ran into issues involving racial stereotypes. Yet I needed to include movies such as *Gone with the Wind*, which are controversial. I faced a similar problem with movies that portrayed negative images of Asian Americans and turned to film historians who discussed the issues and placed the movies in historical context.

For me, research meant not only reading, but the fun of viewing old movies and clips created and performed by the women I presented in this book. Going behind the scenes to understand their work enabled me to realize what women filmmakers had remarkably achieved in the beginning of cinema.

I hope readers will watch and enjoy these vintage movies to see the growth of America's unique art form, motion pictures. And with me, celebrate the phenomenal contributions of the women who built Hollywood.

WHERE TO SEE EARLY HOLLYWOOD FILMS

THE UNITED STATES

The Academy Museum of Motion Pictures, Los Angeles, CA, academymuseum.org

Billy Rose Theatre Division, New York Public Library for the Performing Arts, New York, NY, nypl.org/about/divisions/billy-rose-theatre-division

Billy Wilder Theater, Hammer Museum, Los Angeles, CA, cinema.ucla.edu/billy-wilder-theater

The Criterion Collection, criterion.com

The Department of Cinema Studies & Moving Image Arts, University of Colorado, Boulder, CO, colorado.edu/cinemastudies

Flicker Alley, flickeralley.com

George Eastman Museum, Rochester, NY. Daily screenings in the Dryden Theatre, eastman.org/dryden-theatre

Kansas Silent Film Festival, Topeka, KS, kssilentfilmfest.org

Kino Lorber Films, kinolorber.com

Library of Congress, Collections with Films and Videos, loc.gov

Milestone Film & Video, milestonefilms.com

Museum of Modern Art Film Library, New York, NY, moma.org/collection/
    about/curatorial-departments/film
National Film Preservation Foundation, filmpreservation.org
National Film Registry, loc.gov/programs/national-film-preservation-board/
    film/registry
Newhallywood Silent Film Festival, Santa Clarita, CA, santaclaritaarts.com/
    newhallywood
Open Culture, openculture.com
The Orphan Film Symposium, New York, NY, wp.nyu.edu/orphanfilm
Roxie Theater, Amazing Tales from the Archives, San Francisco, CA,
    roxie.com/ai1ec_event/san-francisco-silent-film-festival-amazing-tales-
    @-the-roxie
San Francisco Silent Film Festival, Castro Theatre, San Francisco, CA
    silentfilm.org
Turner Classic Movies, tcm.com
UCLA School of Theater, Film & Television, Westwood, CA, tft.ucla.edu
Vimeo Video Library, vimeo.com
YouTube, youtube.com

UNITED KINGDOM

Hippodrome Silent Film Festival, Bo'ness, Scotland, hippodromecinema.
    co.uk/silent-film-festival
Yorkshire Silent Film Festival, Yorkshire, England, ysff.co.uk

ITALY

Il Cinema Ritrovato, Bologna, festival.ilcinemaretrovato.it
Pordenone Silent Film Festival organized by Cineteca del Friuli,
    Pordenone, italybyevents,com/en/events/friuli/venezia-giulia/silent-
    film-festival-pordenone

NETHERLANDS

Eye Filmmuseum, Amsterdam, eyefilm.nl/en

Lewis Hine took this photo in May 1910 and titled it,
"Where the boys spend their money. Location: St. Louis,
Missouri."

ACKNOWLEDGMENTS

During the pandemic I told my editor Carolyn Yoder that I wanted to do a book about silent film stars and call it *Girls with Curls*, half thinking she'd be interested. To my surprise, she loved Hollywood and suggested expanding the idea to an anthology that would also include women behind the camera. I thank Carolyn for her enthusiasm and guidance in helping me tell the stories of twelve trailblazers.

My thanks to Barbara Grzeslo, senior art director, Thalia Leaf, associate editor, and the whole team at Calkins Creek/Astra Books for Young Readers.

I greatly appreciate the foreword by Ruth E. Carter with Meera Manek.

A bouquet of thanks to my literary agent, Kevin O'Connor, and to Kristine Krueger, curator at the Academy of Motion Picture Arts and Sciences. I am grateful to film scholar Cari Beauchamp for reading the manuscript for accuracy, and to Hannah Gomez, Ariel Vanece, and Mindy Hsieh for their careful review of tone. A special thank-you to Gregory Mark for his reminiscences, and to Edward Roebuck for his assistance. As always, I am indebted to my critique group—Tony Johnston, Jenny Johnston, Lael Litke, Jane Olson, and Martha Tolles—for their comments and support. I am also grateful to Donald Sosin, silent film musician, for his scores, workshops, and knowledge.

Last, but never least, I thank my husband Michael for living with a compulsive writer all these years.

BIBLIOGRAPHY

BOOKS

Acker, Ally. *Reel Women: Pioneers of the Cinema.* New York: Continuum, 1991.

Affron, Charles. *Lillian Gish: Her Legend, Her Life.* Berkeley, CA: University of California Press, 2002.

Alistair, Rupert. *The Name Below the Title: 65 Classic Movie Character Actors from Hollywood's Golden Age.* Las Vegas: printed by the author, 2018.

Beauchamp, Cari. *Without Lying Down: Frances Marion and the Powerful Women of Early Hollywood.* Berkeley, CA: University of California Press, 1997.

Bogle, Donald. *Bright Boulevards, Bold Dreams: The Story of Black Hollywood.* New York: Ballantine Books, 2005.

———. *Hollywood Black: The Stars, the Films, the Filmmakers.* New York: Running Press, 2019.

Bridges, Melody, and Cheryl Robson, eds. *Silent Women: Pioneers of Cinema.* Twickenham, UK: Supernova Books, 2016.

Brownlow, Kevin. *The Parade's Gone By. . . .* Berkeley, CA: University of California Press, 1976.

———. *Mary Pickford Rediscovered.* New York: Harry N. Abrams in association with the Academy of Motion Picture Arts and Sciences, 1999.

Butchart, Amber. *The Fashion of Film: How Cinema Has Inspired Fashion.* London: Mitchell Beazley, 2016.

Chan, Anthony B. *Perpetually Cool: The Many Lives of Anna May Wong.* Lanham, MD: Scarecrow Press, 2003.

Cho, Jenny, and the Chinese Historical Society of Southern California. *Chinese in Hollywood.* Charleston, SC: Arcadia Publishing, 2013.

Dong, Arthur. *Hollywood Chinese: The Chinese in American Feature Films.* Santa Monica, CA: Angel City Press, 2019.

Finamore, Michelle Tolini. *Hollywood Before Glamour: Fashion in American Silent Film*. New York: Palgrave Macmillan, 2013.

Gish, Lillian, with Ann Pinchot. *The Movies, Mr. Griffith, and Me*. Englewood Cliffs, NJ: Prentice-Hall, 1969.

Gregory, Mollie. *Stuntwomen: The Untold Hollywood Story*. Lexington, KY: University Press of Kentucky, 2018.

Hodges, Graham Russell Gao. *Anna May Wong: From Laundryman's Daughter to Hollywood Legend*. New York: Macmillan, 2004.

Jackson, Carlton. *Hattie: The Life of Hattie McDaniel*. New York: Madison Books, 1990.

Jorgensen, Jay. *Edith Head: The Fifty-Year Career of Hollywood's Greatest Costume Designer*. Philadelphia: Running Press, 2010.

Kirby, Lynne. *Parallel Tracks: The Railroad and Silent Cinema*. Durham, NC: Duke University Press, 1997.

Lim, Shirley Jennifer. *Anna May Wong: Performing the Modern*. Philadelphia: Temple University Press, 2019.

Malone, Alicia. *Backwards & in Heels*. Coral Gables, FL: Mango Publishing, 2018.

Marion, Frances. *Off With Their Heads!: A Serio-Comic Tale of Hollywood*. New York: Macmillan, 1972.

Mayne, Judith. *Directed by Dorothy Arzner*. Bloomington, IN: Indiana University Press, 1994.

McLean, Adrienne L., ed. *Costume, Makeup, and Hair: Behind the Silver Screen*. New Brunswick, NJ: Rutgers University Press, 2016.

Penley, Constance, ed. *Feminism and Film Theory*. New York: Routledge, 1988.

Prichard, Susan Perez. *Film Costume: An Annotated Bibliography*. Metuchen, NJ: Scarecrow Press, 1981.

Regester, Charlene. *African American Actresses: The Struggle for Visibility, 1900–1960*. Bloomington, IN: Indiana University Press, 2010.

Slide, Anthony. *The Griffith Actresses*. Cranbury, NJ: A. S. Barnes, 1973.

Stamp, Shelley. *Lois Weber in Early Hollywood*. Oakland: University of California Press, 2015.

———. *Movie-Struck Girls: Women and Motion Picture Culture After the Nickelodeon*. Princeton, NJ: Princeton University Press, 2000.

Watts, Jill. *Hattie McDaniel: Black Ambition, White Hollywood*. New York: Amistad, 2005.

Whitfield, Eileen. *Pickford: The Woman Who Made Hollywood*. Lexington, KY: University of Kentucky Press, 1997.

Yoo, Paula. *Shining Star: The Anna May Wong Story*. New York: Lee & Low Books, Inc., 2009.

Yuen, Nancy Wang. *Reel Inequality: Hollywood Actors and Racism*. New Brunswick, NJ: Rutgers University Press, 2018.

ARTICLES

Abramovitch, Seth. "Oscar's First Black Winner Accepted Her Honor in a Segregated 'No Blacks' Hotel in L.A." *The Hollywood Reporter*, Feb. 19, 2015. hollywoodreporter.com/features/oscars-first-black-winner-accepted-774335.

Aliperti, Cliff. "Louise Beavers—Biography of Imitation of Life's Aunt Delilah." *Immortal Ephemera*, Mar. 11, 2013. immortalephemera.com/32629/louise-beavers-biography.

Associated Press, "Margaret Booth, Film Editor, 104." *New York Times*. Nov. 2, 2002. nytimes.com/2002/11/02/arts/margaret-booth-film-editor-104.html.

Atkins, Irene Kahn. "Margaret Booth." Interview. *Focus on Film,* vol. 25, summer 1975.

Basinger, Jeanine. "Giving Credit." *DGA Quarterly Magazine*, winter 2011.

Beavers, Karen. "Everybody Has a Mammy: The Productive Discomfort of Louise Beavers' Movie Maids." *Genders*, July 2, 2010. colorado.edu/gendersarchive1998-2013/2010/07/02/everybody-has-mammy-productive-discomfort-louise-beavers-movie-maids.

Bogle, Donald. "The Long Movie Struggle to Shatter Racial Myths." *Philadelphia Tribune*, Nov. 23, 2020.

Booth, Margaret. "The Cutter." *Behind the Screen: How Films Are Made*, edited by Stephen Watts. London: Arthur Barker Ltd., 1938.

Calhoun, Dorothy Donnell. *Motion Picture*, vol. 29, March 1925.

Dargis, Manohla, and A. O. Scott. "She Edited Her Way to Power at MGM." "You Know These 20 Movies. Now Meet the Women Behind Them." *New York Times*, Sept. 20, 2018. nytimes.com/interactive/2018/09/14/movies/women-film-history.html.

Ebert, Roger. "The Birth of a Nation." *RogerEbert.com*, March 30, 2003. rogerebert.com/reviews/great-movie-the-birth-of-a-nation-1915.

Elizabeth S. "Clare West—'Studio Designer.'" *The Classics Café*. Aug. 8, 2020. theclassicscafe.com/post/clare-west-studio-designer.

Freitas, Shirley (great-granddaughter of Helen Holmes). "The Hazardous Life of Helen Holmes." necessarystorms.com/home/the-hazardous-life-of-helen-holmes.

Hauser, Christine. "A Raging Pandemic and a Resistance to Masks: Welcome to 1918." *New York Times*, Aug. 4, 2020.

Kay, Karyn, and Gerald Peary. "Interview with Dorothy Arzner." *Agnes Films*, Jul. 16, 2011. agnesfilms.com/interviews/interview-with-dorothy-arzner.

Kramer, Fritzi. "The Curse of Quon Gwon (1916): A Silent Film Review." *Movies Silently*, Apr. 3, 2016. moviessilently.com/2016/04/03/the-curse-of-quon-gwon-1916-a-silent-film-review.

Lindsay, Kitty. "Forgotten Women of Film History: Marion Wong." *Ms.* Oct. 20, 2014. msmagazine.com/2014/10/20/forgotten-women-of-film-history-marion-wong.

Luther, Claudia. "Margaret Booth, 104; Film Editor Had 70-Year Career." *Los Angeles Times*, Oct. 31, 2002. latimes.com/archives/la-xpm-2002-oct-31-me-booth31-story.html.

"Marion Wong." *Oakland Wiki*. localwiki.org/oakland/Marion_Wong.

McCone, Brigit. "Vintage Viewing: Marion E. Wong Energetic
　　Entrepreneur." *Bitch Flicks*. Sept. 25, 2017. btchflcks.com/2017/09/
　　marion-wong-energetic-entrepreneur.html#.X9U8AS2Z0i4.

Meares, Hadley. "The Thrill of Sugar Hill." *Curbed: West Adams
　　Los Angeles*. la.curbed.com/2018/2/22/16979700/west-adams-history-
　　segregation-housing-covenants.

Perri, Ashlyn, and Momo Chang. "CAAM Co-presents Earliest Known
　　Asian American Film, 'The Curse of Quon Gwon.'" *CAAM* (caamedia.
　　org/blog/author/caamguest/).

Popegrutch, "The Curse of Quon Gwon (1916)." Century Film Project.
　　centuryfilmproject.org/2016/07/23/the-curse-of-quon-gwon-1916.

Sanchez, Chelsey. "Everything to Know about the Real Hattie McDaniel
　　Before Watching *Hollywood*." *Harper's Bazaar*, May 5, 2020.
　　harpersbazaar.com/culture/film-tv/a32380090/who-is-hattie-mcdaniel-
　　hollywood.

Scott, Mike. "Mo'Nique's Oscars Ensemble Pays Tribute to Hattie
　　McDaniel." *Times-Picayune*, March 8, 2010.
　　nola.com/entertainment_life/movies_tv/article_1744cde5-f9f8-576c-
　　b67c-36e55b142762.html.

Spangler, Todd. "HBO Max Restores 'Gone With the Wind' With
　　Disclaimers Saying Film 'Denies the Horrors of Slavery.'" *Variety*.
　　variety.com/2020/digital/news/gone-with-the-wind-hbo-max-
　　disclaimer-horrors-slavery-1234648726.

Stamberg, Susan. "How Movie Darling Mary Pickford Became the Most
　　Powerful Woman in Hollywood." *NPR*, Feb. 27, 2018.
　　npr.org/2018/02/27/589061990/mary-pickford-darling-of-the-silver-
　　screen-to-major-hollywood-force.

tart. *Persephone Magazine*. "Badass Ladies of History: Marion Wong."
　　Persephone Magazine, June 9, 2011 persephonemagazine.
　　com/2011/06/badass-ladies-of-history-marion-wong.

"Way Down East: How Lillian Gish Suffered for Her Art." *Silent London,*
Aug. 19, 2016. silentlondon.co.uk/2016/08/19/way-down-east-how-
lillian-gish-suffered-for-her-art.

West Adams Heritage Association. "Louise Beavers."
westadamsheritage.org/read/478.

SELECTED VIDEOS

Affairs of Anatol/Five Kisses, The aka *Anatol* (1921), Cecil B. DeMille,
costumes by Clare West.

Alice Adams (1935), starring Katharine Hepburn, with Hattie McDaniel.

Big House, The (1930), starring Wallace Beery, script by Frances Marion.

Broken Blossoms (1919), starring Lillian Gish, directed by D. W. Griffith.

Champ, The (1931), starring Wallace Beery and Jackie Cooper, script by
Frances Marion.

Christopher Strong (1933), starring Katharine Hepburn, directed by
Dorothy Arzner.

Coquette (1929), starring Mary Pickford, with Louise Beavers.

Curse of Gwon Quon: When the Far East Mingles with the West, The.
Academy Film Archive, National Film Registry.

Dance, Girl, Dance (1940), starring Lucille Ball and Maureen O'Hara,
directed by Dorothy Arzner, the Criterion Collection, 2020.

Emperor Jones, The (1933), starring Paul Robeson and Fredi Washington.

Foundling, The (1916), starring Mary Pickford, scenario by Frances Marion.

Gone with the Wind (1939), starring Vivien Leigh, Clark Gable, and Hattie
McDaniel.

Hazards of Helen, The. oldies.com, Alpha Video Distributors, 2016.

*Hollywood Chinese: The Chinese in American Feature Films***.** DeepFocus
Productions, hollywoodchinese.com, 2007, 2008, 2010.

Imitation of Life (1934), directed by John Stahl, starring Louise Beavers,
Claudette Colbert, and Fredi Washington.

Intolerance (1916), directed by D. W. Griffith, costumes by Clare West.

Johanna Enlists (1918), starring Mary Pickford, script by Frances Marion.

Little Princess, A (1917), starring Mary Pickford, script by Frances Marion.

Margaret Booth Receives an Honorary Award: 1978 Oscars, youtube.com/watch?v=7eA5MMnROug.

Mutiny on the Bounty (1935), starring Clark Gable and Charles Laughton, edited by Margaret Booth.

My Best Girl (1927), starring Mary Pickford and Buddy Rogers.

Orphans of the Storm (1921), starring Lillian and Dorothy Gish, directed by D. W. Griffith.

Poor Little Rich Girl, The (1917), starring Mary Pickford, script by Frances Marion.

Rebecca of Sunnybrook Farm (1917), starring Mary Pickford, script by Frances Marion.

Red Lantern, The (1919), with Anna May Wong as an extra.

Romeo and Juliet (1936), directed by George Cukor, edited by Margaret Booth.

Scarlet Letter, The (1926), starring Lillian Gish, script by Frances Marion.

Shanghai Express (1932), starring Marlene Dietrich and Anna May Wong.

Show Boat (1936), starring Paul Robeson and Hattie McDaniel.

Tess of the Storm Country (1914), starring Mary Pickford.

Tess of the Storm Country (1922), starring Mary Pickford.

Thief of Bagdad, The (1924), starring Douglas Fairbanks, with Anna May Wong.

This Changes Everything (2019), documentary produced by Ilan Arboleda and Kerianne Flynn, with executive producer Geena Davis.

Toll of the Sea, The (1922), starring Anna May Wong, script by Frances Marion.

Unseen Enemy, An (1912), starring Lillian and Dorothy Gish, directed by D. W. Griffith.

Way Down East (1920), starring Lillian Gish, directed by D. W. Griffith.

Webs of Steel (1926), starring Helen Holmes, Lost Silent Classics Collection. Oldies.com, Alpha Home Entertainment, 2013.

Why Change Your Wife? (1920), directed by Cecil B. DeMille, costumes by
    Clare West.

Wild Party, The (1929), directed by Dorothy Arzner.

Wilful Peggy (1910), starring Mary Pickford, directed by D. W. Griffith.

Yank at Oxford, A (1938), edited by Margaret Booth.

SOURCE NOTES

INTRODUCTION

"The doors . . . to women": Beauchamp, Cari. *Without Lying Down: Frances Marion and the Powerful Women of Early Hollywood.* Berkeley, CA: University of California Press, 1997, p. 12.

"flickers": Affron, Charles. *Lillian Gish: Her Legend, Her Life.* Berkeley, CA: University of California Press, 2001, p. 44.

"a complete disgrace": Whitfield, Eileen. *Pickford: The Woman Who Made Hollywood.* Lexington, KY: The University of Kentucky Press, p. 61.

"Temples of . . . Silent Drama": Ibid., p. 141.

CHAPTER 1

"During a . . . my parts": Brownlow, Kevin. *Mary Pickford Rediscovered.* New York: Harry N. Abrams in association with the Academy of Motion Picture Arts and Sciences, 1999, p. 22.

"the girl . . . curls": Malone, Alicia. *Backwards & in Heels: The Past, Present, and Future of Women Working in Film.* Coral Gables, FL: Mango Publishing Group, 2018, p. 36.

"America's Sweetheart": Ibid., p. 37.

"innocent babies": Whitfield, p. 22.

"There was . . . did it": Ibid., p. 48.

"When I saw . . . for them": Ibid., p. 50.

"We'll have . . . Mary Pickford": Ibid., p. 55.

"a promising future": Ibid., p. 61.

"Oh, no . . . family together": Ibid., p. 64.

"golden curls . . . too fat": Ibid., p. 75.

"the thing . . . her face": Beauchamp, Cari. "Mary Pickford Joins Biograph." Cari Beauchamp articles. Mary Pickford Foundation, marypickford.org/caris-articles/mary-pickford-joins-biograph.

"wardrobe": Whitfield, p. 77.

"distinctly bad": Ibid., p. 79.

"I made . . . no kissing": Ibid., p. 87.

"the Great Unkissed": Ibid., p. 92.

"The movie . . . thinking": Ibid., p. 88.

"I learned . . . the theater": Slide, Anthony. *The Griffith Actresses*. South
    Brunswick and New York: A. S. Barnes and Company, 1973, p. 66.

"She was . . . information": Beauchamp, Cari. "Mary Pickford Joins
    Biograph," p. 2.

"There is . . . camera": Brownlow, Kevin. *Mary Pickford Rediscovered*, p. 67.

"like a . . . head off": Ibid., p. 67.

"an ingénue . . . attention": Slide, *The Griffith Actresses*, p. 67.

"the girl . . . curls": Nicholson, Amy. "Mary Pickford: The Woman Who
    Shaped Hollywood." *The Women Who Changed Cinema*. Feb. 4,
    2019. bbc.com/culture/article/20190204-mary-pickford-the-woman-
    who-shaped-hollywood.

"Little Mary": Whitfield, p. 112.

"Mary . . . *Storm Country*": Ibid., p. 130.

"that was . . . career": Brownlow, *Mary Pickford Rediscovered*, p. 91.

"Daily Talks": Beauchamp, *Without Lying Down*, p. 63.

"It must . . . people's love": Brownlow, p. 20.

"I am . . . girl myself": Brownlow, p. 32.

"Mary Pickford . . . 'Grown Up'": *New York Times*, June 23, 1928.

"They're gone . . . and Pollyanna forever": Beauchamp articles, pages 1–2
    of marypickford.org/caris-articles/mary-cuts-her-hair.

"her unique . . . industry": 48th Academy Awards Memorable Moments,
    Oscars Ceremonies, 1976.

"They don't . . . the public": Whitfield, p. 370.

"The only great art": Ibid., p. 370.

"I didn't . . . my parts": Brownlow, p. 22.

CHAPTER 2

"Griffith always . . . of people": Slide, *The Griffith Actresses*, pp. 97–98.

"Of the . . . ethereal beauty": Affron, Charles. *Lillian Gish: Her Legend, Her Life*. Berkeley, CA: University of California Press, 2001, p. 45.

"He was . . . a king": Gish, Lillian with Ann Pinchot. *The Movies, Mr. Griffith, and Me*. Englewood Cliffs, NJ: Prentice-Hall, 1969, p. 35.

"Red, you . . . wonderful scene": Gish, *The Movies, Mr. Griffith, and Me*, p. 37.

"wordless acting . . . weird": Affron, p. 52.

"disappeared . . . insecurity . . . on me": Gish, p. 6.

"'Aunt' Alice": Ibid., p. 7.

"We had . . . loved it": Ibid., p. 1.

"The problem . . . with us": Ibid., p. 15.

"a very . . . on the side": Affron, p. 57.

"The films . . . the players": Gish, p. 84.

"Don't act . . . feel it": Ibid., p. 87.

"make the . . . an audience": Lillian Gish, interview, *The Dick Cavett Show*, 1971. youtu.be/ZOPY_8Gch-4.

"Everything planned . . . craftsmen": Affron, p. 127.

"snobbishness.": Ibid., p. 63.

"the creation . . . form.": Lillian Gish, interview, *The Dick Cavett Show*, 1971. youtu.be/ZOPY_8Gch-4.

"Two Famous Sisters": Gish, p. 112.

"won her . . . of people": Slide, p. 98.

"household word": Gish, p. 114.

"We had . . . the day": Gish, p. 138.

"During parts . . . so moving": Affron, p. 82.

"*The Birth* . . . twentieth century": Bogle, Donald. *Bright Boulevards, Bold Dreams: The Story of Black Hollywood*. New York: One World, 2005, p. 13.

"the birth of an art": James Agee quoted in Ebert, "*The Birth of a Nation*," March 30, 2003, p. 2.

"Have been . . . and dying": Affron, p. 111.

"I was . . . to care": Gish, p. 219.

"a masterpiece . . . pictures": Affron, p. 130.

"It was . . . picture": Ibid., p. 131.

"dumbfounded . . . You know . . . pictures": Gish, p. 223.

"unhug": Affron, p. 137.

"Would never . . . woman is": Ibid., p. 138.

"helpless heroine": Slide, p. 95.

"*Get that face!*": Gish, p. 233.

"This kind . . . and perfect": Ibid., p. 234.

"Lillian . . . for Griffith": Ibid., pp. 236–237.

"I can't . . . your own": Ibid., p. 247.

"I began . . . at all": Affron, p. 145.

"the perfect girl": Ibid., p. 161.

"a *very* serious actress": Ibid., p. 161

"The faces . . . the words": "Lillian Gish—from Silent Films to TV specials."
    The Christian Science Monitor, Feb. 13, 1981, p. 1.
    csmonitor.com/1981/0213/021300.html.

"It was . . . technical century": Academy Awards speech, 1971.

CHAPTER 3

"I owe . . . women": Malone, p. 46.

"If I . . . my job": Beauchamp, p. 22.

"You've got the looks": Ibid., p. 30.

"The movie . . . cockeyed business": Marion, Frances. *Off With Their
    Heads!: A Serio-Comic Tale of Hollywood*. New York: Macmillan, 1972,
    p. 8.

"Were the . . . stay": Ibid., p. 6.

"Would you . . . starlets?": Beauchamp, p. 37.

"How soon . . . start?": Ibid., p. 37.

"a new . . . women": Ibid., p. 42.

"have fun together": Ibid., p. 43.

"This started . . . writing": Rogers St. Johns, Adela. "Frances Marion: The Cosmopolite of the Month." *Cosmopolitan*, May 1945, p. 3.

"I ceased . . . earth": Beauchamp, p. 45.

"A good . . . seem important": Ibid., p. 45.

"Applause . . . a hit!": Marion, p. 44.

"Although . . . an audience": Ibid., p. 45.

"special . . . Pickford": Beauchamp, p. 70.

"The screen . . . pace": Ibid., p. 176.

"It is . . . our screen stories": Marion quoted in Petersen, Elizabeth Benneche, "Great Women of Motion Pictures," *Screenland* 38, no. 3, (January 1939).

"The awfulness . . . they endured": Beauchamp, p. 96.

"Give the . . . least like": Frances Marion's Screen Writing Forum." *How to Write and Sell Film Stories*. Reviewed by James Boothe, *Cinema Progress*, 1937/1938, p. 35.

"champion of . . . to the screen": Beauchamp, p. 176.

"We see . . . grey dress": Ibid., p. 177.

"dialogue writers": Marion, Frances. *Off With Their Heads!*, New York: Macmillan, 1972, p. 185.

"the results . . . overacted": Marion, *Off With Their Heads!*, p. 186.

"I hope . . . endless": Beauchamp, p. 370.

"I owe . . . women": Malone, p. 46 and Beauchamp, p. 12.

CHAPTER 4

"I am . . . them": Regester, Charlene. *African American Actresses: The Struggle for Visibility, 1900–1960*. Bloomington, IN: Indiana University Press, 2010, p. 103.

"perfected . . . the day": Bogle, Donald, quoted in Regester, p. 75.

"the African . . . people": Ibid., p. 73.

"In all . . . except savages": Ibid., p. 74.

"*Pal of* . . . I don't . . . I was": Ibid., p. 73.

"slave at wedding": *Uncle Tom's Cabin* (1927), Full Cast & Crew, IMDb.

"We play . . . and classes": Aliperti, p. 3.

"I've worked . . . domestic service": Bogle, Donald. *Bright Boulevards, Bold Dreams: The Story of Black Hollywood*. New York: One World Books, 2006, p. 152.

"race movies": Bogle, Donald, *Hollywood Black: The Stars, The Films, The Filmmakers*. New York: Running Press, 2019, p. 9.

"up-lift": Regester, p. 99.

"I am . . . live them": Ibid., p. 103.

"her . . . Californian": Eileen Creelman quoted in Aliperti, p. 6.

"I had . . . foreign language": Regester, p. 104.

"white . . . dialect": Ibid., p. 91.

"warmth and . . . vulnerability": Bogle, *Bright Boulevards, Bold Dreams*, p. 129.

"became so . . . she lived" Regester, p. 104.

"Put this . . . the year": Aliperti, p. 21.

"notable work": Ibid., p. 21.

"the real . . . Delilah": Regester, p. 98.

"Miss Beavers . . . person": *Madera Tribune*, vol. LXV, number 46, December 27, 1934.

"The Academy . . . Black!": Regester, p. 98.

"because . . . too good": Jimmie Fidler quoted in Aliperti, p. 21.

"I'd rather . . . be one": Alistair, Rupert. *The Name Below the Title: 65 Classic Movie Character Actors from Hollywood's Golden Age*. Las Vegas: published by the author, 2018, p. 33.

"First Lady . . . triumph": Aliperti, p. 15.

"It is . . . Constitution": Meares, Hadley. "The Thrill of Sugar Hill." *Curbed Los Angeles*, February 22, 2018, p. 8. la.curbed.com/2018/2/22/16979700/west-adams-history-segregation-housing-covenants.

"black stardom": Regester, p. 6.

"to honor . . . Black people": Abraham, Dixie. *California Aggie*, vol. 91, no. 26, February 11, 1976. UCR Center for Bibliographical Studies and Research. CDNC, California Digest Newspaper Collection.

CHAPTER 5

"I am . . . it": Washington quoted by Earl Conrad, "Pass or Not to Pass?"
   Chicago Defender, June 16, 1945.

"No matter . . . a Negro": Ibid.

"a young . . . of Negro blood": Bogle, *Bright Boulevards*, p. 128.

"Noted . . . on record": Ibid., p. 128.

"distinct . . . intelligence": Ibid., p. 129.

"There are . . . my fingers": Ibid., p. 134.

"I don't . . . the movies": Ibid., p. 135.

"I didn't . . . Broadway . . . dim-witted maid . . . in now": Ibid., p. 135.

"They just . . . race": Ibid., p. 135.

"And if . . . paper": Ibid., p. 135.

"I always . . . *opportunities*": Ibid., p. 137.

"vital . . . earnest": Ibid., p. 122.

"Fredi . . . could have voiced": Ibid., p. 122.

"I have . . . do so": Ibid., p. 123.

"In Imitation . . . my race": Ibid., p. 124.

"Peola . . . to 'pass'": Ibid., p. 122.

"Why should . . . to do": Ibid., p. 123.

"splendid . . . picture offers": Bogle, p. 152.

"A Man . . . Yesterday" The New Negro Movement, the NAACP Flag.
   loc.gov/exhibits/naacp/the-new-negro-movement.html, p. 5.

"frail . . . by day": Regester, p. 125.

"Who said . . . to stay": Ibid., p. 129.

"using her . . . social justice": Ali, Rasha. "Regina King talks 'bittersweet'
   success amid COVID-19, protests as one of Glamour's Women of the
   Year" *USA Today*, October 11, 2020.

"As a Black . . . been through . . . hope . . . attention": Regina King
   quoted by Catherine Wright, "Regina King on the Black Lives
   Matter Movement." *Home/Celebrity*, October 16, 2020, pp. 1 and 3.
   cheatsheet.com/entertainment/regina-king-on-the-black-lives-matter-
   movement-were-at-our-true-reckoning.html.

CHAPTER 6

"I'm a . . . my house": Watts, Jill. *Hattie McDaniel: Black Ambition, White Hollywood.* New York: HarperCollins, 2005, p. 132.

"Hattie, I'll . . . shouting again": Jackson, Carlton. *Hattie: The Life of Hattie McDaniel.* New York: Madison Books, 1990, p. 9.

"I always . . . public": Watts, p. 31.

"I recall . . . a story": Jackson, p. 9.

"Convict Joe": Ibid., p. 11.

"There is so much . . . people happy": Watts, p. 34.

"a means . . . honest dollar": Ibid., p. 36.

"Boo Hoo Blues": Ibid., p. 64.

"I landed . . . broke": Ibid., p. 74.

"I never . . . job": Ibid., p. 75.

"types": Ibid., p. 81.

"A call . . . home": Ibid., p. 83.

"was one . . . met": Ibid., p. 122.

"a very . . . dresser": Ibid., p. 132.

"I'm a . . . my house": Ibid., p. 132.

"is treated . . . dignity": Ibid., p. 155.

"brilliant performance": Jackson, p. 47.

"stood and . . . McDaniel": Ibid., p. 52.

"one of . . . my life": Ibid., p. 52.

"Black . . . ecstatic": Bogle, *Bright Boulevards*, p. 183.

"to aim . . . hard": Jackson, p. 54.

"I consider . . . personal progress": Watts, p.180.

"This moment . . . been opened": Halle Berry, Academy Awards acceptance speech, Mar. 24, 2002; Kodak Theatre. *Academy Awards Acceptance Speech Database.*

"I want . . . have to": Mo'Nique, *Academy Awards Acceptance Speech Database*, 2009 Academy Awards, March 7, 2010, Kodak Theatre.

"Miss Hattie . . . over me": Mo'Nique, *Celebrity Greeks: Highlighting Famous Members of the Divine Nine*, March 29, 2010, p. 2. celebritygreeks.blogspot.com/2010/03/monique-honors-actress-hattie-mcdaniel.html.

CHAPTER 7

"I decided . . . China": *Oakland Wiki, Oakland Tribune*, May 11, 1917, quoted, p. 2. localwiki.org/oakland/Marion_Wong.

"They Must Go": Chang, Iris. *The Chinese in America*. New York: Penguin Books, 2003. Illustration for advertisement of pest control, "Rough on Rats." Chinese Historical Society of America, San Francisco.

"I had . . . the world": *Oakland Tribune*, May 11, 1917, quoted in *Persephone Magazine*, p. 3. persephonemagazine.com/2011/06/badass-ladies-of-history-marion-wong. Also, *Oakland Wiki*, p. 2. localwiki.org/oakland/Marion_Wong.

"imagination . . . beauty": McCone, Brigit. *Bitch Flicks*, September 25, 2017, p. 2. btchflicks.com/2017/09/marion-wong-energetic-entrepreneur.html.

"Princess . . . Song Bird": Dong, Arthur. *Hollywood Chinese: The Chinese in American Feature Films*. DeepFocus Productions, 2019, Los Angeles: Angel City Press, p. 223.

"I first . . . love story": Dong, *Hollywood Chinese*, p. 223.

"Then, I decided . . . a success": Ibid., pp. 223–224.

"working for . . . republic": Ibid., p. 224.

"*The Curse* . . . civilization": Mark, Gregory Yee. "The Curse of Quon Gwon: Chinese America's Pioneering Film." *Early Cinematic Experience of Hong Kong, Book III, Re-Discovering Pioneering Females in Early Chinese Cinema*, Grandview's Cross-Border Productions, p. 209.

"Los Angeles . . . drama" "Badass Ladies of History: Marion Wong.": *Persephone Magazine*, June 2, 2011. persephonemagazine.com/2011/06/badass-ladies-of-history-marion-wong.

"Oriental": Anna May Wong quoted in Dong, p. 143.

"lost face": Author's phone conversation with Gregory Yee Mark, August 4, 2021.

"Gregory . . . it": Mark, Gregory Yee. "The Curse of Quon Gwon: Chinese America's Pioneering Film," p. 212.

"Three . . . film": Author's phone conversation with Gregory Yee Mark, August 4, 2021.

CHAPTER 8

"I would . . . too": Chan, Anthony B., *Perpetually Cool: The Many Lives of Anna May Wong*. Lanham, MD: Scarecrow Press, 2007, p. 29.

"It made . . . in May": Ibid., p. 16.

"Chink . . . Chinaman.": Ibid., p. 17.

"We lived . . . fright": Ibid., p. 18.

"We were . . . picture": Ibid., p. 28.

"C.C. . . . Child": Malone, p. 65.

"Yes, I . . . too": Chan, p. 29.

"The studio . . . too long": Chan, p. 31.

"to witness . . . at all": Ibid., p. 32.

"You have . . . play hooky": Hodges, Graham Russell Gao. *Anna May Wong*. New York: Palgrave Macmillan, p. 18.

"Your eyes . . . work hard": Chan, p. 31.

"I am . . . go unnoticed": Hodges, p. 23.

"Of course . . . in China": Chan, p. 138.

"Anna . . . your soul": Ibid., p. 36.

"completely . . . the screen": Malone, p. 66.

"demure butterfly": *Wikipedia*, "Anna May Wong." en.org/wiki/Anna_May_Wong.

"Yellowface": Chan, p. 39, Hodges, p. 57, Malone, p. 67.

"No film . . . the man": Ibid., p. 67.

"entrancing . . . good": Chan, p. 212.

"Anna . . . delight": Ibid., p. 214.

"A good . . . actress": Hodges, p. 25.

"There are . . . Chinese parts": Chan, p. 39.

"Anna . . . her go": Ibid., p. 48.

"her . . . a double": Ibid., p. 52.

"Why is . . . of honor": Ibid., p. 68.

"You're asking . . . characters": Yuen, Nancy Wang. *Reel Inequality: Hollywood Actors and Racism*. New Brunswick, NJ: Rutgers University Press, 2018, p. 123.

"real Chinese . . . my fathers": Chan, p. 90.

"All I . . . told me": Ibid., p. 92.

"This . . . career": Ibid., p. 99.

"I was . . . art": Ibid., p. 97.

"I hoped . . . light": Ibid., p. 117.

"Many women . . . a machine!": Ibid., p. 123.

"A rhythm . . . essence of it" Wong quoted in Leung, Louise, "East Meets West," *Hollywood Magazine*, January 1938, p. 40.

"I was . . . that process": Desta, Yohana. "Lucy Liu Pays Tribute to Anna May Wong During Touching Walk of Fame Ceremony." *Vanity Fair*, May 2, 2019, vanityfair.com/hollywood/2019/05/lucy-liu-walk-of-fame-speech.

CHAPTER 9

"I wanted . . . a woman": Mayne, Judith. *Directed by Dorothy Arzner*. Bloomington and Indianapolis: Indiana University Press, 1994, p. 55.

"I had . . . familiar to me": Kay, Karyn, and Gerald Peary. "Interview with Dorothy Arzner." *Agnes Films*, July 16, 2011, p. 2.

"It was . . . or knowledge": Kay, pp. 2–3.

"If one . . . what to do": Ibid., p. 3.

"At the bottom": Ibid., p. 3.

"A good . . . editor": Ibid., p. 3.

"I worked . . . loved it": Mayne, p. 25.

"There's nothing . . . every minute": Arzner quoted in interview with Kevin
     Brownlow. Bridges, Melody, and Cheryl Robson, eds. *Silent Women:
     Pioneers of Cinema*. Twickenham, UK: Supernova Books, 2016, p. 193.
"I'd rather . . . for Paramount": Kay, p. 6.
"Paramount's first woman director": Mayne, p. 35.
"If fashion . . . make them": Brownlow, Kevin, *The Parade's Gone
     By* . . . Berkeley, CA: University of California Press: 1968, p. 286.
"what her . . . to do": Mayne, p. 37.
"star-maker": Ibid., p. 49.
"the only . . . her job": Ibid., p. 156.
"No director . . . with me": Ibid., p. 51.
"was up . . . skin on!": Ibid., p. 9.
"Talking to . . . Strong.": Ibid., p. 9.
"*Christopher Strong* . . . the time": Ibid., p. 10.
"to find. . . film history": Mayne, p. 5.
"I was . . . it was a woman": Ibid., p. 55.
"She wasn't . . . enormous heart": *Dorothy Arzner*. UCLA Film and
     Television Archive, cinema.ucla.edu/collections/dorothy-arzner.
"There was . . . performers are doing . . . the actors": Ibid.
"You'll make . . . encouragement": Ibid.
"To be . . . me walk out" Dorothy Arzner, AZ Quotes. azquotes.com/
     author/75380-Dorothy_Arzner.

CHAPTER 10

"In the . . . like poetry": Margaret Booth quoted in Atkins, Irene Kahn.
     "Margaret Booth." *Focus on Film*, vol. 25, summer 1975, p. 51.
"When I . . . put together": Ibid., p. 51.
"went to . . . playing": Ibid., p. 51.
"didn't . . . work meant": Ibid., p. 51.
"It was . . . work": Brownlow, p. 303.

"greater importance": Booth quoted in Hatch, Kristen, "Cutting Women: Margaret Booth and Hollywood's Pioneering Female Film Editors." Women Film Pioneers Project, p. 4.

"He taught . . . how to edit": Brownlow, p. 302.

"I was . . . at night . . . to him": Atkins, p. 52.

"I used . . . the rhythm": Brownlow, p. 303.

"I would count . . . right tempo": Hatch, p. 4.

"When you . . . like poetry": Atkins, p. 51.

"good picture": Booth, Margaret. "The Cutter." *Behind the Screen: How Films Are Made*, edited by Stephen Watts. London: Arthur Barker Ltd., 1938, p. 148.

"was really the cutter": Atkins, p. 52.

"I enjoyed . . . everyone": Brownlow, p. 303.

"I knew . . . family studio": Ibid., p. 303.

"We were . . . was terrifying": Ibid., p. 304.

"At first . . . in sync": Atkins, p. 52.

"electronic people": Ibid., p. 52.

"throw the . . . any way": Hatch, p. 5.

"the boy wonder": "Irving Grant Thalberg," *Encyclopaedia Britannica*. britannica.com/biography/Irving-Thalberg.

"he was . . . in pictures": Brownlow, p. 303.

"How do . . . a woman?": Booth, Margaret. "The Cutter," p. 150.

"It was . . . close-up": Atkins, p. 53.

"Every time . . . of operations": Ibid., p. 54.

"I used . . . cut it": Ibid., p. 54.

"It was wonderful": Ibid., p. 54.

"savagely . . . very best": "*Mutiny on the Bounty*." en.wikipedia.org/wiki/Mutiny_on_the_Bounty (1935 film).

"The picture . . . *Bounty*": Atkins, p. 55.

"It's a . . . see": Ibid., p. 55.

"I enjoyed . . . at that": Ibid., p. 54.

"I was . . . lovely trip": Ibid., p. 55.

"Directors . . . finish it": Brownlow, p. 305.

"quite different . . . done rhythmically": Atkins, p. 55.

"I don't . . . to tell": Ibid., p. 57.

"Isn't it . . . to do?": "Margaret Booth Receives an Honorary Award: 1978 Oscars," youtube.com/watch?v=7eA5MMnR0ug.

"I think . . . editors today": Thelma Schoonmaker, *Fresh Air* interview with Terry Gross, NPR, May 31, 2005.

"We don't . . . the audience": Thelma Schoonmaker quoted in, Bushby, Helen, "Martin Scorsese's Editor Thelma Schoonmaker on His Hatred of Eyebrows." BAFTA Awards, Jan. 25, 2020.

CHAPTER 11

"The screen . . . the style!": Clare West quoted in "Read How Paris Copies Styles Set by Hollywood," *Motion Picture*, March 1925, p. 111.

"head of wardrobe": *International History of Costume Design.* filmreference.com/encyclopedia/Academy-Awards-Crime-Films/ Costume-INTERNATIONAL-HISTORY-OFCOSTUME-DESIGN.html.

"to suit its . . . always loved . . . my career!": Clare West quoted in Owston-Booth, Dorothy. "The Career of Clare." *Pictures and Picturegoer,* April 1923, pp. 24–25.

"costume design . . . obtainable": Finamore, Michelle Tolini. *Hollywood Before Glamour: Fashion in American Silent Film.* New York: Palgrave Macmillan, 2013, p. 124.

"Madame Clare . . . Fine Arts studio": *Motion Picture News*, March–April 1916, p. 1471.

"studio designer": McLean, Adrienne, ed. *Costume, Makeup, and Hair.* New Brunswick, NJ: Rutgers University Press, 2016, p. 27.

"I had . . . their freshness": Clare West quoted in Owston-Booth, "The Career of Clare," pp. 24–25.

"Back to . . . Fashions": *Photoplay*, April 1917 quoted in McLean, p. 29.

"larger than life clothing": "Clare West." *Women Film Pioneers Project.* wfpp.columbia.edu/pioneer/ccp-clare-west.

"I want . . . in a store": Butchart, Amber Jane, *The Fashion of Film: How Cinema Has Inspired Fashion*, Hachette, UK, September 8, 2016, p. 68.

"playing . . . store": Butchart, p. 68, and Finamore, p. 124.

"I have . . . to me": Owston-Booth, "The Career of Clare," p. 25.

"You must . . . to wear": Clare West quoted in Fletcher, Adele Whitely. "Tales Out of School," *Pictures and Picturegoer*, July 1925, p. 41.

"That Octopus Gown": *Photoplay*, 1921, p. 20.

"I try . . . the character": West quoted by Fletcher, "Tales Out of School," p. 41.

"the wickedest . . . dangerous to men": Clare West quoted in *Photoplay*, 1921, p. 20.

"feel": Author interpreting quote in *Motion Picture News*, August 1921, January 1922, p. 44.

"One must . . . the screen": West quoted in Owston-Booth, "The Career of Clare," p. 25.

"The screen . . . the style!": West quoted in *Motion Picture*, March 1925.

"The American . . . and London": West quoted in "Copied From Films," *Moving Picture World*, March 3, 1923.

"Cutting edge styles": McLean, p. 29.

"Sometimes . . . a picture": West quoted in Fletcher, "Tales Out of School."

"Beautiful gowns . . . heroine": Calhoun, Dorothy Donnell. *Motion Picture*, March 1925, p. 137.

"I find . . . a mood": Ruth E. Carter quoted in Ward, Beth. "'Black Panther' Designer Ruth E. Carter Fashions Portals to Then, Now and the Future." *Arts ATL*, February 2, 2021, p. 5. artsatl.org/author/beth-ward.

CHAPTER 12

"If I want . . . in myself": Freitas, Shirley. "The Hazardous Life of Helen Holmes," necessarystorms.com/home/the-hazardous-life-of-helen-holmes.

"damsel in distress": Ibid., p. 6 of 21.

"the Railroad Girl": York, Cal. "Plays and Players." *Photoplay*, 1919, p. 86. And Freitas, p. 2.

"motoring skills": Gregory, Mollie. *Stuntwomen: The Untold Story.* Lexington, KY: University Press of Kentucky, 2015, p. 10.

"Votes for Women": *Past Forward: Activating the Henry Ford Archive of Innovation.* "The Automobile and Women's Suffrage," by Saige Jedele, Assistant Curator, August 25, 2020, p. 4 of 9. thehenryford.org/explore/blog/the-automobile-and-women-s-suffrage.

"Helen controls . . . passengers": Freitas, p. 8 of 21.

"Racing-driver . . . may require": *Photoplay Magazine*, January 1916, p. 108.

"It was . . . make a series!": "Helen Holmes Is Still an Active Player." *Photoplay* 1924.

"Nearly all . . . thrilly action . . . write it myself": Holmes quoted in Stamp, Shelley. *Movie-Struck Girls.* Princeton: Princeton University Press, 2000, p. 145.

"dainty figure . . . worries her": Stamp, p. 146.

"Helen . . . her biceps": Freitas, p. 6 of 21.

"a mass . . . iron": Ibid., p. 10 of 21.

"women . . . they want": Kirby, Lynne. *Parallel Tracks: The Railroad and Silent Cinema.* Durham, NC: Duke University Press, 1997, p. 111.

"terrible wreck": Mahar, Karen Ward. "Helen Holmes." *Women Film Pioneers Project.* wfpp.columbia.edu/pioneer/ccp-helen-holmes.

"There are . . . the pants": Malone, p. 50.

"Today's . . . actresses": Gregory, p. 24.

"In her . . . a hero": Malone, p. 50.

AFTERWORD: WOMEN IN HOLLYWOOD TODAY

"Women virtually . . . film era": Tietjen, Jill S. and Barbara Bridges. *Hollywood: Her Story*. Lanham, MD: Lyons Press, 2019.

"Talent and . . . not gender": Ibid., p. 2.

"Emulating . . . multitasking": Ibid., p. 26.

"Today women . . . under represented": Cari Beauchamp. caribeauchamp. com/contact.

"Discrimination . . . exists": Maria Giese quoted in *This Changes Everything*, directed by Tom Donahue in association with the Geena Davis Institute on Gender in Media, 2018.

"We can . . . better": Ava DuVernay quoted in Bob Straus, "Ava DuVernay on directing 'A Wrinkle in Time' and other breakthroughs in show-biz diversity." *New York Daily News*, March 2, 2018.

"The future . . . female": Malone, p. 242.

INDEX

Page numbers in **boldface** refer to images and/or captions.

PICTURE CREDITS

Alamy: 41, 44, 65, 154, 157, 161.

Black Film Center/Archive, Indiana University, Bloomington, IN: 60.

George Eastman Museum: 35, 78, 160.

Getty: 95.

Library of Congress:
  LC-USZ62-97197: 34,
  LC-DIG-ggbain-23327: 58,
  LC-USZ62-135273: 106,
  LC-DIG-nclc-04666: 172.

Los Angeles Times Photographic Archive, UCLA Library Digital Collections: 88.

Margaret Herrick Library: 17, 22, 24, 26, 28, 47, 50, 52, 64, 74, 82, 93, 111, 112, 130, 142, 150, 158.

Photofest: 1, 12, 23, 40, 42, 49, 67, 69, 72, 76, 90, 92, 114, 116, 120, 126, 128, 132, 138, 139 (left), 139 (right), 145, 147, 148, 151.

United States Mint: 168.

University of Southern California Libraries, Charlotta Bass/ California Eagle Photograph Collection, 1870-1960: 87.

The Violet Wong Family Collection and *Hollywood Chinese: The Chinese in American Feature Films*: 96, 100, 102–103, 104.